Moyo,

Don't stop declaring.
congratulations er manyfektor

GODFESSIONS 3

'Goke Coker

West African Version

Published by AuthorHouse 04/24/2018

ISBN: 978-1-5462-3993-2 (sc)
ISBN: 978-1-5462-3992-5 (hc)
ISBN: 978-1-5462-3991-8 (e)

Print information available on the last page.

Any people depicted in stock imagery provided by Getty Images are models, and such images are being used for illustrative purposes only.
Certain stock imagery © Getty Images.

This book is printed on acid-free paper.

ACKNOWLEDGEMENTS

I would like to express my heartfelt gratitude to all my Blackberry Messenger Contacts who have endured the daily broadcasts of this international piece, whose encouragements and response have contributed to the development of this book project, fast evolving into a brand.

A very big thank you to Omowonuola, Adeyeoluwa and Obademilade, My darling wife and our adorable daughters, for your sacrifice and support and for consistently giving me the much needed space to pursue the vision. I love you.

Roland, Sesan, Aisha and Dele, your encouragement at different times have been priceless. The value of your confirmation of the "next step" and interest in the project can never be overemphasised. Thank you for your contribution.

To Jumoke Ariyo, Jackson Tugbeh, Tolu Akinbami, and Steve Harris, you represent a very long list of people who commended the consistent effort of daily confession and its transformation into a devotional. Your responses to the positive impact of those prayers have gone a very long way in the development of this piece and the birth of a brand.

Abiola "Champ" Salami, thanks for the connection with AuthorHouse. John Zedomi, Gbenga Oluwole, and Tiriah David-West, your feedback kept me going when I felt like giving up. Those telephone calls came in the nick of time.

A very special thanks to Julius Artwell and the entire AuthorHouse family for the excellent and professional services they have so graciously provided and for making time through the process.

I'm so grateful to God for my spiritual parents and Pastor, The Rev'd Paul and Ifeanyi Adefarasin. Thank you for taking the time to teach, train tutor and mentor me through the years, and thank you for the opportunity to serve. I couldn't have asked for better. Thanks Mum and Dad.

Also to Damilola, Yinka and Dayo Sanya, Ayo and Bimpe, Yomi and Tayo, Faith Nwosu, Wale Oyedeji, The El Bernards, Charlotte & Belinda, Kemi Balogun, Kene, Nkechi, Christabel, Frances, Phoebe, EvaMarie, Omilola, Modupe, Oscar and Titi.

And to my family - Mum and Dad, Florence Abimbola and David Adeyemi Coker.

Siblings-Adenike, Adebisi, Adekunle "KC" Adedoyin and Folashade, Adetokunbo and Adebanji. I am forever grateful.

DEDICATION

In loving memory of
Chief Magistrate Akinrinde Oluwayemisi Akinola.
(1935 - 1979)
Though I didn't get the opportunity of meeting you, I am
thankful for the amazing gift of your daughter, Omowonuola.

&

My Aunt
Mrs Mojirade Oyawe
(1943 - 2017)

Contents

INTRODUCTION

Words have presence, power, and prophetic implications. Words have life. Jesus said in John 6:63, "The Words that I speak to you, they are spirit and they are life." Words are the only creative force of life. With words we create, re-create, change, prohibit, and allow things in our lives. This is the power of confession.

Words have no geographical limitations, they can penetrate anything and anywhere. A Roman centurion said to Jesus in Matthew 8:8, "I am not worthy that thou should come under my roof; but speak the word only and my servant shall be healed". He understood that Gods word could be spoken anywhere and still produce result.

Confession means "to repeatedly and continually say a thing in order to achieve a desired end." Confession also means; "The affirmation of truth." Anyone can make a confession irrespective of age, gender, race, creed, or location - anyone who desires to repeatedly affirm a truth or a conviction towards a desired end.

There are any perceived truths in the world that people subscribe to and confess, but only the truth of God's word will make a man free indeed. So when we confess Gods word, we set in motion the power of true freedom in our lives.

Words are more important than a lot of people realize. We must recognize the place that confession holds in the scheme of things. Jesus himself showed us the power of our words when he said in Matthew 17:20, "Ye shall say unto this mountain, Remove hence to yonder place; and it shall remove; and nothing shall be impossible unto you." The Message Bible says "You could do anything! Jesus is showing words have presence, power and prophetic and prophetic implication. Words have life. Jesus said in John 6:63, "The words that I speak to you, they are spirit and they are life."

1. Called and Chosen

Today, I speak over my life and my household that the newness of Gods grace will shine upon us and that Gods mercy attaches itself to us all the days of my life.

I bask in the sea of Gods steadfast love, I receive the peace of His glorious presence, and Im surrounded by the hosts of heaven; I will not fear, because God is with me. I am a city sought after; I am favored by men, and God has set me apart for miracles for the rest of my life. My future is clear, and I cannot be stranded. My progress is steady, I will not be delayed, I am accepted in the beloved, and I will never be rejected. I have been selected and elected, called, and chosen; I am a city on a hill, and my glory cannot be hidden. I am ordained for greatness; I break the yoke of smallness and shatter the chains of mediocrity. I have life; I am blessed with abundance, and I partake of the divine nature. I have life eternal. I take my place among the elders at the gate. I am an ambassador of Gods kingdom. I am a carrier of the divine spirit. I am a child of consolation and a son of encouragement. I am programmed for dominion and primed for greatness. I was born to rule, and I was created to reign in life. I prosper. I am a creature of immense value, made for glory and honor. I am the apple of Gods eye; I am the salt of the earth and the light of the world. I am one of a kind. I am the Kings son. Everything works for my good.

In Jesuss name, I believe and say amen.

Selected Affirmations

I am a creature of immense value, made for glory and honor.

I am favored by men, and God has set me apart for miracles for the rest of my life.

Suggested Scriptures

Everyone that is called by my name: for I have created him for my glory, I have formed him; yea, I have made him. (Isaiah 43:7)

And Jesus increased in wisdom and stature, and in favor with God and man. (Luke 2:52)

Whereby are given unto us exceeding great and precious promises: that by these ye might be partakers of the divine nature, having escaped the corruption that is in the world through lust. (2 Peter 1:4)

And God said, Let us make man in our image, after our likeness: and let them have dominion over the fish of the sea, and over the fowl of the air, and over the cattle, and over all the earth, and over every creeping thing that creeps upon the earth. (Genesis 1:26)

2. Rest without Fear

Today, I speak over my life and my household that God will set a hedge of protection around us and keep us safe from hurt and harm.

I am surrounded by the hosts of heaven, like mountains surround Jerusalem. I lift the shield of faith, and I douse every fiery dart of the enemy. God is my buckler and my strong tower, a mighty fortress and my high tower; He is my impenetrable bunker, a no-go zone for the enemy. I will not fear what my foes may do or say, for I am loved by God. Perfect love casts out fear, and I do not have the spirit of slavery again to fear; I have the spirit of power, I have the spirit of love, and I have a sound mind. The Lord is my light, and the Lord is my strength; He is my portion, and He is my salvation. I will be afraid of no one, for I am the redeemed of the Lord, and I belong to Him. I have been bought with the blood of the everlasting covenant; He gave His commandment and charge concerning me, so I must not be harmed. I am the anointed of the Lord, set apart for His divine and holy use. I am untouchable to the enemy of my soul; I am kept jealousy as the apple of His eye. My soul rests without inhibition, and my heart dwells in safety. I am not moved, my gaze is fixed on the most high, and I will not see shame. My hands are lifted high in triumph over my enemies, and all my foes are destroyed.

In Jesuss name, I believe and say amen.

Selected Affirmations

He gave His commandment and charge concerning me, so I must not be harmed. I am the anointed of the Lord, set apart for His divine and holy use.

Suggested Scriptures

No man taketh it from me, but I lay it down of myself. I have power to lay it down, and I have power to take it again. This commandment have I received of my Father. (John 10:18)

And he said unto his men, The LORD forbid that I should do this thing unto my master, the LORDS anointed, to stretch forth my hand against him, seeing he is the anointed of the LORD. (1 Samuel 24:6)

For we are his workmanship, created in Christ Jesus unto good works, which God hath before ordained that we should walk in them. (Ephesians 2:10)

The LORD is my light and my salvation; whom shall I fear? the LORD is the strength of my life; of whom shall I be afraid? (Psalm 27:1)

3. Living in the Realm of All Possibilities

Today, I speak over my life and my household that God has come through for us. I encounter His power on a daily basis.

I see the miraculous manifestation of His grace constantly. His mercies are new every morning; I am not exempt from the loving kindness of the Lord my God. I am sanctified unto good works by the God of heaven and earth. Angels excel in strength, and they minister to me; they have charge over me so I walk in confidence. He hears my every prayer; God cannot deny me, and I am distinguished by His favor and blessed by His righteous right hand. I dwell in the realm of all possibilities, and darkness flees before me. God sustains me, His mercy meets me, and His compassion finds me. My situation is turned around. I am lifted; I am sorted. Things are working for me, and nothing is against me. He rules and reigns over my life, and my steps are ordered by Him. I am directed into favor, and breakthroughs wait at every turn in my life. I am a sign and a wonder unto many. God is in control of my life, and nothing will get out of hand; I have peace like a river. I am an amazement to my foes, and I am an outstanding personality created as a pointer to Gods intention for the reconciliation of humankind to Himself. I attain destiny and purpose. God has raised me above all my peers. I am too blessed to be stressed; I am too graced to be cursed. There is no condemnation. I have been justified. God loves me.

In Jesuss name, I believe and say amen.

Selected Affirmations

I am an outstanding personality created as a pointer to Gods intention for the reconciliation of humankind to Himself.

I encounter His power on a daily basis. I see the miraculous manifestation of His grace constantly.

Suggested Scriptures

And all things are of God, who has reconciled us to himself by Jesus Christ, and has given to us the ministry of reconciliation. (2 Corinthians 5:18)

Verily my house is not so with God; Yet he hath made with me an everlasting covenant, Ordered in all things, and sure. (2 Samuel 23:5)

The steps of a good man are ordered by the LORD: and he delights in his way. (Psalm 37:23)

Far above all principality, and power, and might, and dominion, and every name that is named, not only in this world, but also in that which is to come. (Ephesians 1:21)

4. Created for Dominion

Today, I speak over my life and my household that God has remembered us for good and that He honors His covenant to us.

I am a victor and victorious in life. I am not alone; God is with me to lead me on the path of righteousness for His namesake. I am blessed and lifted, and all things are possible to me because I believe. My faith receives a boost today as always, and God moves me to the front from the rear. I am not restricted or held back, for every chain of limitation is broken and I attain the very best in God for my life. I prosper in all my hands find to do. Every ability and endowment from God in me finds expression. I am an addition to this generation, and I have the mind of Christ. I have the wisdom of God; light shines on my path, and I am upheld by the power of His spirit. I am not stagnant; I move forward, I press onward, and I am motivated and encouraged. I stop at nothing, my goals are achievable, and my dreams are alive; God favors me, and men honor me. I overcome every giant standing on my way to success, I topple every negative mind-set, I have a mind-expanding encounter, and I am an agent of positive change. I am born to reign and created for dominion; greatness is attracted to me. I win always, and everything is working for me. I am divinely assisted and supernaturally supported. My generation will hear about me. I am strong for the fight and distinguished in victory. I am elevated and lifted. Its my time. I am blessed above the rest.

In Jesuss name, I believe and say amen.

Selected Affirmations

Every ability and endowment from God in me finds expression.

I have the mind of Christ. I have the wisdom of God; light shines on my path, and I am upheld by the power of His spirit.

Suggested Scriptures

For which I also labor, striving according to his working, who works in me mightily. (Colossians 1:29)

For who has known the mind of the Lord, that he may instruct him? But we have the mind of Christ. (1 Corinthians 2:16)

6 However, we speak wisdom among those who are mature, yet not the wisdom of this age, nor of the rulers of this age, who are coming to nothing. 7 But we speak the wisdom of God in a mystery, the hidden wisdom which God ordained before the ages for our glory. (1 Corinthians 2:67)

Your word is a lamp unto my feet, and a light unto my path. (Psalm 119:105)

5. Fruitfulness

Today, I speak over my life and my household that Gods grace and peace is multiplied over our lives and that His mighty power imparts change and works wonders in our lives today.

I am a source of wonder to many; I bring succor to many and solutions to creations problem. I operate under open heavens, and I break through on all sides. I am a planting in the garden of the Lord by the rivers of His living water; my leaves shall never wither, my branch shall remain in strength, and I bring forth fruit in every season. God is my covering and shield; He is my fortress and my strong tower. The Lord, my God, is mighty to save. He is my song in the times of weariness, my banner in the days of battle. I shall never be moved; I remain established in the secret place of the most high, and I firmly abide under the shadow of the Almighty. I have the peace of God that is beyond human understanding. God is with me; nothing offends me. God is for me, and nothing is against me. God has justified me, and none condemn me. I am free from the law of sin and death; the spirit of life in Christ Jesus operates in me. I partake of the divine nature. Life favors me. Grace gets me over at all times. I enjoy the loving kindness of the Lord. I enter into a new season. I experience the newness of Gods grace and glory. He perfects everything that concerns me. I live above fear. I am settled for life and eternity. I rise above challenges, situations, and circumstances.

In Jesuss name, I believe and say amen.

Selected Affirmations

God is with me, and nothing offends me. God is for me, and nothing is against me. God has justified me, and none condemn me.

I am a planting in the garden of the Lord by the rivers of His living water; my leaves shall never wither, my branch shall remain in strength, and I bring forth fruit in every season.

Suggested Scriptures

Devise your strategy, but it will be thwarted; propose your plan, but it will not stand, for God is with us. (Isaiah 8:10)

For I know nothing against myself; yet am I not thereby justified: but he that judges me is the Lord. (1 Corinthians 4:4)

Who was delivered for our offenses, and was raised again for our justification. (Romans 4:25)

Those that are planted in the house of the LORD shall flourish in the courts of our God. (Psalm 92:13)

6. Substitutionary Sacrifice

Today, I speak over my life and my household that God will show us mercy like He promised and that we have favor everywhere we turn.

I lift the cup of the blood of the lamb shed from before the foundation of the earth; I lift the broken body and declare Passover! The angel of death passes over my house and family, for I invoke the power of the substitutionary sacrifice and enter into the season of supernatural favor instead of death. I have dancing for mourning, the garment of praise for the spirit of heaviness, beauty for ashes, and joy unspeakable for sackcloth. I call in a bountiful harvest and sustained increase. I activate the Fathers will and appropriate the fullness of His blessings. My bread is blessed, and my water is blessed. I will not cast my young. Sickness and disease the Lord has taken away from my family, and I fulfill the number of my days. He fights for me. I hold my peace, and I turn my enemies away in disgrace. I enter into the season of new beginnings; I am a part of the performing generation. My life matters. God is my light. My eyes are filled with light. There is no darkness around me. God shows me kindness everywhere. I go forward; I get more than I bargained for. I have the spirit of power, might, and a sound mind. I am like Christ; I have the mind of Christ.

In Jesuss name, I believe and say amen.

SELECTED AFFIRMATIONS

I enter into the season of supernatural favor instead of death. I have dancing for mourning, the garment of praise for the spirit of heaviness, beauty for ashes, and joy unspeakable for sackcloth.

SUGGESTED SCRIPTURES

You shall arise, and have mercy upon Zion: for the time to favor her, yea, the set time, is come. (Psalm 102:13)

You have turned for me my mourning into dancing: you have put off my sackcloth, and girded me with gladness. (Psalm 30:11)

To appoint unto them that mourn in Zion, to give unto them beauty for ashes, the oil of joy for mourning, the garment of praise for the spirit of heaviness; that they might be called trees of righteousness, the planting of the LORD, that he might be glorified. (Isaiah 61:3)

Whom having not seen, ye love; in whom, though now ye see him not, yet believing, ye rejoice with joy unspeakable and full of glory. (1 Peter 1:8)

7. Peace beyond Understanding

Today, I speak over my life and my household that the peace of God that surpasses understanding will garrison across our hearts.

I am not shaken nor moved. I trust in God completely. I lean not on my own understanding; I acknowledge Him in all my ways, and I am directed of the Lord and led by the Spirit. I see my way through; I walk a path devoid of pitfalls. I look to the Lord my God, and I will not see shame. I am delivered from destruction and dereliction. I am saved to serve and strengthened for life. God is merciful to me, and I have received grace of the Lord my God. I have favor. Nothing is against me. Men are favorably disposed to me in every situation. I am accepted and not rejected. Nothing blocks my path to success; I am not a failure, and greatness is attracted to me. I activate the will of the Father and insist that today is the day of His power. I am willing; God is at work, in me, to will and to do all His good pleasure. I win always. My prayers are answered, and my requests are granted. My eye is single, and my body is full of light. Sorrows and tears are far from me. I have peace; my struggles cease; my frustrations, fears, and frailties give way; and I am strong in the Lord and in the power of His might. My tomorrow is greater and better than my yesterday. I shine like the star that I am. I am blessed with every blessing heavenly, in heavenly places in Christ Jesus. I am blessed with the blessing of the sand and stars. I increase on all sides.

In Jesuss name, I believe and say amen.

Selected Affirmations

Men are favorably disposed to me in every situation.

I activate the will of the Father and insist that today is the day of His power.

Suggested Scriptures

And Jesus increased in wisdom and stature, and in favour with God and man. (Luke 2:52)

Thy people shall be willing in the day of thy power, in the beauties of holiness from the womb of the morning: thou hast the dew of thy youth. (Psalm 110:3)

No weapon that is formed against you shall prosper; and every tongue that shall rise against you in judgment you shall condemn. This is the heritage of the servants of the LORD, and their righteousness is of me, says the LORD. (Isaiah 54:17)

Finally, my brethren, be strong in the Lord, and in the power of his might. (Ephesians 6:10)

8. Newness of Life

Today, I speak over my life and my household that God has opened a new chapter in the story of our lives and that a new thing begins in us today.

I enter into the newness of life, and I experience the power of God like never before. His steadfast love remains a constant and ceaseless flow in my direction; I see His goodness in the land of the living, and the splendor of His glory upon my life shows me off in new light. I am a fresh discovery to mankind, I get my due from creation, and I receive divine favor like never before. The might of the Lord encompasses me; I am protected just like the apple of His eye. The Lord my God is with me; He fights my battle for me, so I hold my peace. The light of His countenance from His word reflects His heart and mind. I walk and wont ever stumble. I have the revelation of His person and the power of His presence; I have fullness of joy. I am anointed with fresh oil; I am selected to do good works. I am the zenith of His creation; I have been lifted to another level and new dimension. I am blessed till I am a blessing; I abide in blessedness. My eyes behold mighty things; I am the elect of the Lord. I go forward only; I am a prince of power with the Lord. I am sustained from the storehouses of heaven; I know no lack, I shall not want, and I am connected to the Father of all flesh. I am strictly under the watch of the angels. I have no need that has not been met according to the riches in glory in Christ Jesus. I am settled financially, emotionally, spiritually, and otherwise. I have testimony superior to that of my enemies. My case is different, and God cares for me. I am a new creation.

In Jesuss name, I believe and say amen.

Selected Affirmations

The splendor of His glory upon my life shows me off in new light; I am a fresh discovery to mankind.

I have been lifted to another level, a new dimension. I am blessed till I am a blessing, I abide in blessedness, and my eyes behold mighty things.

Suggested Scriptures

Declare his glory among the nations, His marvellous works among all the peoples. (1 Chronicles 16:24)

And they shall be upon thee for a sign and for a wonder, and upon thy seed for ever. (Deuteronomy 28:46)

11 Being enriched in every thing to all bountifulness, which causeth through us thanksgiving to God.
12 For the administration of this service not only supplieth the want of the saints, but is abundant also by many thanksgivings unto God. (2 Corinthians 9:1112)

Though he fall, he shall not be utterly cast down: for the LORD upholdeth him with his hand. (Psalm 37:24)

9. Grace for the Race

Today, I speak over my life and my household that God is a covering for us in the day of trouble and our ever-present help in times of need.

Because He is my fortress, I will never be shaken. I put my trust in God; I will not see shame and disgrace. I am loved perfectly, so fear is defeated, and I rise above every inhibition and striving of the tongue. Greater is He that is inside me than he that is the world. I am kept safe and secure in Him, by the power of His name, I am protected. His blood speaks better things on my behalf. The hedge of protection around me is sure, so I break through the camp of the enemy and walk in divine victory all the days of my life. I speak peace to every tossing of the sea and boisterous wind action in my space. I declare nothing missing and nothing broken in my life. All is at rest; there is calm from the eye of the storm. God is king over the storm; He rules over every area of my life. I have the keys of David; I release the ability of the Holy Spirit and the wisdom of God most high. I am complete in Him. I see light in His light. He is beautiful for my situation, and He makes all things beautiful in His time. He works in me both to will and to do His good pleasure. I have a willing Spirit to walk with in the blessing of His household. Today is the beginning of the day of His power. I move forward in life, I have grace for my race, and I am crowned with plenty of crowns. Good things must happen to me. My harvest is plentiful, and it comes in now! My basket of abundance overflows with Gods bounties. I do not miss out. I move into a wealthy place.

In Jesuss name, I believe and say amen.

Selected Affirmations

I am loved perfectly, so fear is defeated, and I rise above every inhibition and striving of the tongue. Greater is He that is inside me than he that is the world. I speak peace to every tossing of the sea and boisterous wind action in my space.

Suggested Scriptures

To the praise of the glory of his grace, in which he has made us accepted in the beloved. (Ephesians 1:6)

Ye are of God, little children, and have overcome them: because greater is he that is in you, than he that is in the world. (1 John 4:4)

And he arose, and rebuked the wind, and said unto the sea, Peace, be still. And the wind ceased, and there was a great calm. (Mark 4:39)

You have caused men to ride over our heads; we went through fire and through water: but you brought us out into a wealthy place. (Psalm 66:12)

10. Vindicated by Grace

Today, I speak over my life and my household that the Lord remembers His covenant toward us and fulfills all His promises made to us.

I am not forsaken, and I am not forgotten; I am one of the chosen few from the many that are called. I am justified, my election is sure, and I am vindicated by the grace of forgiveness and the cleansing power of His blood. Everything is brand-new. I am led by the Holy Ghost. I have the spirit of adoption; He is my Father, I have the inheritance of sons, and I am an heir of God and joint heir with Christ. I win always because the Lord fights my battle. I cannot lose out in the game of life because God is for me and nothing can be against me. Everything is working for my own good. I love God, and He loved me first. I am called according to His purpose. I am purchased by the blood; I do not own myself. I am redeemed for the top. I am reconciled for greatness: I succeed, I prevail, I am promoted, and I am the response to Gods plan for the restoration of humanity. I am accepted in the beloved. I walk in health, I abide in peace, and I profit and prosper in all I do. I remain a sign and wonder to my generation. I come through the fire and the flood. I take my place in life. I reign as a king priest. Nothing can stop me.

In Jesuss name, I believe and say amen.

Selected Affirmations

I am justified, my election is sure, and I am vindicated by the grace of forgiveness and the cleansing power of His blood.

I am redeemed for the top. I am reconciled for greatness: I succeed, I prevail, and I am promoted.

Suggested Scriptures

Therefore being justified by faith, we have peace with God through our Lord Jesus Christ. (Romans 5:1)

Wherefore the rather, brethren, give diligence to make your calling and election sure: for if ye do these things, ye shall never fall. (2 Peter 1:10)

7 In Him we have redemption through His blood, the forgiveness of sins, according to the riches of His grace 8 which He made to abound toward us in all wisdom and prudence. (Ephesians 1:78)

And we know that in all things God works for the good of those who love him, who have been called according to his purpose. (Romans 8:28)

11. Free Indeed

Today, I speak over my life and my household that God has given us the victory, the enemy is defeated, and we are triumphant.

The walls of limitation are destroyed, the chains of stagnation are broken, and the heavy baskets of retrogression are shatteredI am free. I operate outside the box. Life has a new meaning. I win always, I cannot be held back, I am jet-propelled into the future, and I break through on all sides. God fights my battles as He promised. I am delivered from the grip of the enemy, and I am not a slave to the wiles of my adversaries. I am free from the law and the power of sin; I am not bound by the fears of men. I break free from the influence of the striving of the tongues of men; I am safe from the conspiracies of men who do not have faith. The Son of God has set me free. I am free indeed. I step into my season of promotion, prosperity, and power. These are my days of miracles and wonder; its the beginning of my weeks and months. I step into unprecedented favor, I walk into abundant life, and I enter into grace so amazing. Things have changed, and good things are happening to me. My joy is full, for I am lifted to the place where I belong. I am upheld by the righteous right hand of the Lord most high. Gods eyes are on me to keep me in safety. He is my strong tower and my fortress, He is my banner of victory and the covering of my head in the days of battle, and He is my help in the times of weariness. I am blessed by God at all times. I will not be shaken. I am blessed above the rest.

In Jesuss name, I believe and say amen.

Selected Affirmations

I am delivered from the grip of the enemy, I am not a slave to the wiles of my adversaries, and I am free from the law and the power of sin.

Suggested Scriptures

If the Son therefore shall make you free, you shall be free indeed. (John 8:36)

Therefore you are no more a servant, but a son; and if a son, then an heir of God through Christ. (Galatians 4:7)

For the law of the Spirit of life in Christ Jesus has made me free from the law of sin and death. (Romans 8:2)

Far above all principality, and power, and might, and dominion, and every name that is named, not only in this age, but also in that which is to come. (Ephesians 1:21)

Surely there is no enchantment against Jacob, neither is there any divination against Israel: according to this time it shall be said of Jacob and of Israel, What hath God wrought! (Numbers 23:23)

12. Preserved Inheritance

Today, I speak over my life and my household that God opens a new chapter of blessings for us and that its the start of new things, a brand-new day.

Power issues forth from heaven for my sake; every barrier is broken, and I am propelled into greatness. The everlasting mercies of the Most High prevail over judgment, and the voice of the blood of the eternal covenant speaks in my favor. Nothing holds me down; I am set at liberty by the decree of the holy angels of God, who excel in strength on my behalf. The word of God concerning my life comes to pass as the Lord my God commandsI have divine acceleration, I have the overtakers anointing and I run past the chariots and the horses. My lot is maintained, and my inheritance is preserved. I have my due in my season; I will not be denied what is mine. I am fortified and protected in battle; I am triumphant in every area of life. I march on without fear; every curse is reversed, and the opposite will happen. I am blessed with every spiritual blessing in heavenly places in Christ Jesus. I have come into the fullness of the blessing of the Abrahamic covenant. The light shines for me; the darkness losses its place. I am not confused, and I see my way through. My name is great, I have global relevance, and my generations are the blessed of the earth. I am lifted forever. I have reward for the service with my God. As I say it, I shall see it.

In Jesuss name, I believe and say amen.

Selected Affirmations

The everlasting mercies of the most high prevails over judgment; the voice of the blood of the eternal covenant speaks in my favor.

I am blessed with every spiritual blessing in heavenly places in Christ Jesus. I have come into the fullness of the blessing of the Abrahamic covenant.

Suggested Scriptures

For he shall have judgment without mercy, that hath shewed no mercy; and mercy rejoiceth against judgment. (James 2:13)

20 Now the God of peace, that brought again from the dead our Lord Jesus, that great shepherd of the sheep, through the blood of the everlasting covenant, 21 Make you perfect in every good work to do his will, working in you that which is well pleasing in his sight, through Jesus Christ; to whom be glory for ever and ever. Amen. (Hebrews 13:2021)

Blessed be the God and Father of our Lord Jesus Christ, who hath blessed us with all spiritual blessings in heavenly places in Christ. (Ephesians 1:3)

That the blessing of Abraham might come on the Gentiles through Jesus Christ; that we might receive the promise of the Spirit through faith. (Galatians 3:14)

13. The Burden Is Lifted

Today, I speak over my life and my household that every conspiracy of hell against us will not see the light of day and that every psychic command spoken against us is turned around like a boomerang to hit right back at its source.

Every weapon formed and fashioned against me shall not prosper; they wont work. I rise up and condemn every tongue that rises against me in judgment. The Lord does not approve of subverting me in my course. The Lord has not put more on me than I can bear; the weight has been taken from my wait. I lay down every heavy burden; I pick up His light weight. I run my race unencumbered. God prevents me from resting the rod of the wicked in my bosom. I will not falter, I will not fall, I will not fail, and I will not put my hands into inequity. I part ways with the company of the scornful, hateful, and those whose pathways lead to destruction. I am the righteousness of God in Christ Jesus, and my paths shine brighter to a perfect day. My name is written down with those who press on to the saving of their soul. I am blessed beyond the curse; I am too blessed to be stressed. I am victorious, I am raised a champion, and I am an amazement to those who know me; I prevail despite the odds against me. I was born great, I am attracted to success, and I have the Fathers blessing. I am encompassed by the hosts of heaven, and I walk in grace and divine favor; I am accepted in the beloved. Things work for me. I am a person of genuine and positive global impact and prominence.

In Jesuss name, I believe and say amen.

Selected Affirmations

The Lord has not put more on me than I can bear; the weight has been taken from my wait. I lay down every heavy burden; I pick up His light weight. I run my race unencumbered.

Suggested Scriptures

And it shall come to pass in that day, that his burden shall be taken away from off thy shoulder, and his yoke from off thy neck, and the yoke shall be destroyed because of the anointing. (Isaiah 10:27)

Come unto me, all you that labor and are heavy laden, and I will give you rest. (Matthew 11:28)

I press toward the mark for the prize of the high calling of God in Christ Jesus. (Philippians 3:14)

But ye are come unto mount Zion, and unto the city of the living God, the heavenly Jerusalem, and to an innumerable company of angels. (Hebrews 12:22)

14. Value Added

Today, I speak over my life and my household that God breaks every barrier of limitation over every area of our existence and shatters every factor of hindrance around us.

I walk away from every wall of stagnation and break through every obstacle from the past set to checkmate the establishment of my glorious destiny. Chains snap, burdens lift, and yokes break; the anointing of the spirit of the living God breaks the shackles of mediocrity constraining my life. I am entrenched in the spirit of excellence, I exceed every expectation, and I am distinguished amongst my peers. My life is a testimony of an outstanding walk with God; I am set aside as the workmanship of the God of heaven. I am gifted and marked for global prominence, my branch spreads over and across the wall, and I am a person of impact in my generation. I grow in wisdom greatly; I am not static in my reasoning. I am an addition to creation, value added to creation. God perfects all that concerns me, and I am the righteousness of God in Christ Jesus. My path is clear; I walk in the fullness of my rights and privileges as joint heir with the Son. My citizenship is in heaven. I am not limited by the law of sin and death. I have the grace of the spirit of life in Christ Jesus at work in my life; I have the Holy Spirit at work inside me. My body is quickened, and I abide in health; sickness, disease, ailments, and infirmity are destroyed. Life, abundant life, and eternal life are freely dispensed to me by the power of the resurrected King of Glory. I reign in life, live in hope, walk in faith, move in victory, rule in authority, and stand in power. I was born in love. God is on my side always. I cant lose.

In Jesuss name, I believe and say amen.

SELECTED AFFIRMATIONS

I am entrenched in the spirit of excellence, I exceed every expectation, and I am distinguished amongst my peers. My life is a testimony of an outstanding walk with God.

SUGGESTED SCRIPTURES

Then this Daniel was preferred above the presidents and princes, because an excellent spirit was in him; and the king thought to set him over the whole realm. (Daniel 6:3)

For surely there is a future hope; and your expectation shall not be cut off. (Proverbs 23:18)

According as he has chosen us in him before the foundation of the world, that we should be holy and without blame before him in love. (Ephesians 1:3)

The LORD make his face shine upon you, and be gracious unto you. (Numbers 6:25)

15. Lifted Gloriously

Today, I speak over my life and my household that the manifold grace of God flows freely to us and that God will show us supernatural favor in every direction we turn.

I have been selected for the glorious lifting of the most high; I am marked for promotion, and God selects me for a new blessing. I step into my seasonits my turn and my time. I am confirmed for comfort, and my turnaround time has come. I shine in the midst of the darkness, the glorious brightness of my light will not grow dim, and I wax brighter to a perfect day. I grow in grace and increase in faith; I manifest the power of Gods spirit. I walk in Gods wisdom, I am full of counsel and might, and I am blessed with the spirit of the fear of God. I have the blessing of a long and healthy life, my path drips honey and butter, and the abundance of the heathen and the hidden riches of secret places are converted to me. My ways are pleasing to God; my enemies are at peace with me. I am a blessing to the world and a source of encouragement to creation. I will eat the good of the land, and my mouth will be filled with the pleasantries of the nations. I know no lack. I lend to nations. I will not borrow. My children are dandled on my knees. Life delivers its sweetness. I have my mate. I will not lack any comfort. My needs are met from the abundance of Gods storehouses. I am provided for bountifully. Heaven supports me.

In Jesuss name, I believe and say amen.

Selected Affirmations

I grow in grace, I increase in faith, and I manifest the power of Gods spirit. I walk in Gods wisdom, I am full of counsel and might, and I am blessed with the spirit of the fear of God. I have the blessing of a long and healthy life, my path drips honey and butter, and the abundance of the heathen and the hidden riches of secret places are converted to me.

Suggested Scriptures

And the child Samuel grew, and was in favor both with the LORD, and also with men. (1 Samuel 2:26)

But grow in grace, and in the knowledge of our Lord and Saviour Jesus Christ. To him be glory both now and forever. Amen. (2 Peter 3:18)

When a mans ways please the LORD, he maketh even his enemies to be at peace with him. (Proverbs 16:7)

Length of days is in her right hand; and in her left hand riches and honour. (Proverbs 3:16)

16. Not Forsaken

Today, I speak over my life and my household that God will neither leave nor forsake us and that the power of His presence will make a difference in our lives.

I run through a troop and leap over a wall; my fingers are trained to bend bows of steel, and my sword is not without blood. I make an impact in life and get positive results in all that I do. I am strong for the battle, and my victory is of the Lord. God fights for me. I have the wisdom of God; because He is ever with me, I am wiser than the ancients. My God is of the ancient days, so I have more wisdom than my peers. The power that controls the heaven and the earth dwells in me; my ways are directed by the spirit of the living God. I am justified by faith; I am accepted in the beloved. I have fullness of joy; I have the blessings of eternal pleasures. I am not rejected, I am content in the presence of my King, and I have peace all around. Because He is always with me, I have the comfort of the sheep with the shepherd. I have life, I have the full expressions of His undying love, and I increase in the revelation of His power and might. Mountains melt and dissolve before me. The seas and storms of life are quieted, for God is ever with me. God has not left me. I am stronger than my foes; I am triumphant. I walk around confidently, men favor me, angels do my bidding, the earth yields her best, and heaven honors my cry. God exceeds my expectation, new things spring forth, and fresh territories are conquered. God surprises me daily with His blessings.

In Jesuss name, I believe and say amen.

Selected Affirmations

The power that controls the heaven and the earth dwells in me. My ways are directed by the spirit of the living God.

Because He is always with me, I have the comfort of the sheep with the shepherd.

Suggested Scriptures

Ye are of God, little children, and have overcome them: because greater is he that is in you, than he that is in the world. (1 John 4:4)

Thy word is a lamp unto my feet, and a light unto my path. (Psalm 119:105)

Be strong and courageous. Do not be afraid or terrified because of them, for the Lord your God goes with you; he will never leave you nor forsake you. (Deuteronomy 31:6)

Show me a sign for good; that they who hate me may see it, and be ashamed: because you, LORD, have helped me, and comforted me. (Psalm 86:17)

17. The Power to Prosper

Today, I speak over my life and my household that God is glorified in us and that the weight of His manifest glory is revealed in us for all eyes to behold.

Gods covenant of wealth is activated in my life; I receive the power to prosper in all my hands find to do according to His spoken promises. I activate angelic assistance and divine support; I am directed by the power of the Holy Spirit. I transcend every earthly limitation and insist that the Kingdom of God has been established in my life and insist that the will of God be done in my life. I superimpose Gods best over every area of my life; Jesus rules over my life, and I yield to the Lordship of the Christ of God and the King of Glory. I am firmly established in His love. I am covered by His absolute power, so my life is worth living, my tomorrow is better than my yesterday, and every day is an addition. I get more than I bargained for; God always exceeds my expectation, and the goodness I receive from God is never lacking. His faithfulness lifts my head by grace, not by the works of my hands. I am blessed exceedingly, abundantly, and far above all that I could ever ask or imagine, according to the glorious power at work inside me. I am set apart for His tender mercies to be seen in my life. His light and life shine through. I am a channel of blessing to many. My life is a positive influence to many. God upholds me with the righteousness of His right hand. I will not fall. I move up to another level. Everything is possible for me. I walk into a life of limitless possibilities.

In Jesuss name, I believe and say amen.

Selected Affirmations

The goodness I receive from God is never lacking. His faithfulness lifts my head by grace, not by the works of my hands. I am blessed exceedingly, abundantly, and far above all that I could ever ask or imagine, according to the glorious power at work inside me.

Suggested Scriptures

The LORD shall open unto you his good treasure, the heaven to give the rain unto your land in its season, and to bless all the work of your hand: and you shall lend unto many nations, and you shall not borrow. (Deuteronomy 28:12)

Now unto him that is able to do exceeding abundantly above all that we ask or think, according to the power that worketh in us. (Ephesians 3:20)

Draw nigh to God, and he will draw nigh to you. Cleanse your hands, ye sinners; and purify your hearts, ye double minded. (James 4:8)

But know that the LORD hath set apart him that is godly for himself: the LORD will hear when I call unto him. (Psalm 4:3)

18. Unhindered Progress

Today, I speak over my life and my household that Gods unfailing hand is upon us and that His unending love differentiates us from the rest of the world.

I am the beloved of the Lord; grace, goodness, mercy, and peace are multiplied to me in the love of the Lord. I am accepted in the beloved. Justified by His blood, I am a covenant child. God is so good to me, and the blessings of the Lord that makes one rich in all things without sorrow are mine. I dwell in a place so secure in the shadow of His wings. I walk in dominion; nothing holds me down, nothing stops my progress, and I go forward unhindered. I am a joint heir with the Son; I have a godly heritage, and my inheritance is secured. God is my source, and I walk in the abundance of the fullness of His love. I walk in the miraculous power of the most high. Life and health, wisdom and counsel are signs of my time. I am elevated and lifted high above my peers, I am jet-propelled from the back to the front, I am empowered by the spirit of the Lord, and I can do all things through Christ, who strengthens me. Nothing is impossible for me, for I am a believer. I break forth and break through on all grounds; the heavens are opened unto me. I hear God expressly, so I am not in the dark. Light shines on my path, and I walk in the covenant of greatness. God is merciful to me; I have unprecedented favor. I have maximum impact in all my undertaking and full yield for all my effort. The earth gives me her best. God moves on my behalf. I am unstoppable; nothing prevents me from my goals. I break away from every resistance, I do not go empty, and God is my source. My faith overcomes the world.

In Jesuss name, I believe and say amen.

SELECTED AFFIRMATIONS

I walk in dominion; nothing holds me down, nothing stops my progress, and I go forward unhindered.

Nothing is impossible for me, for I am a believer. I break forth and break through on all grounds.

SUGGESTED SCRIPTURES

Thou madest him to have dominion over the works of thy hands; thou hast put all things under his feet. (Psalm 8:6)

Jesus said unto him, If thou canst believe, all things are possible to him that believeth. (Mark 9:23)

I can do all things through Christ which strengtheneth me. (Philippians 4:13)

And the LORD shall make thee the head, and not the tail; and thou shalt be above only, and thou shalt not be beneath; if that thou hearken unto the commandments of the LORD thy God, which I command thee this day, to observe and to do them. (Deuteronomy 28:13)

19. Hidden in Christ Jesus

Today, I speak over my life and my household that God is our shield and exceedingly great reward, our fortress, and our ever-present help in the time of need.

I am not without comfort. God is my strength and my salvation; I am protected by the power of the Holy Spirit. The name of the Lord is a strong tower; I find safety as I run into it. I am hidden in Christ and in God; no harm shall befall me and my family. My confidence is in the Lord the maker of the earth and creator of the universe. I rest in the faithfulness of my Father and my King; He is my fortress. I will never be shaken, for I look to Him and will never be put to shame. I trust in God, and I will never be disgraced. God is for me, and nothing is against me. I am established in the covenant, and I find fulfillment in the love of God. Grace promotes me to where condemnation cannot demote me. God is my keeper, and the Lord is my light. He is ever with me; no weapon formed or fashioned against me shall prosper, and every tongue that rises against me is condemned. I am delivered from the striving of the tongue of men; I am covered by God from the insurrection of the enemy. The conspiracy of hell against me is destroyed. I abide eternally under the shadow of the Almighty; I say that the Lord is my refuge and my fortress. With the dawn of the day, the sun of righteousness arises over me with healing in its wings. With the balm of Gilead, my wounds are healed. With the Prince of Peace, nothing is missing and nothing is broken in my life. It is well with me and my family. I go forward, I go upward, and I find rest in God. I am accepted in the beloved. Gods love is revealed and made manifest in my life.

In Jesuss name, I believe and say amen.

Selected Affirmations

I am hidden in Christ and in God, and no harm shall befall me and my family. Grace promotes me to where condemnation cannot demote me.

God is my keeper, and the Lord is my light. He is ever with me; no weapon formed or fashioned against me shall prosper, and every tongue that rises against me is condemned.

Suggested Scriptures

For ye are dead, and your life is hid with Christ in God. (Colossians 3:3)

For by grace are ye saved through faith; and that not of yourselves: it is the gift of God. (Ephesians 2:8)

The LORD is thy keeper: the LORD is thy shade upon thy right hand. (Psalm 121:5)

No weapon that is formed against thee shall prosper; and every tongue that shall rise against thee in judgment thou shalt condemn. This is the heritage of the servants of the LORD, and their righteousness is of me, saith the LORD. (Isaiah 54:17)

20. I Abide in His Love

Today, I speak over my life and my household that Gods love abides with us and that His loving kindness is our portion.

I am protected and have found His mercy; I am forgiven and released. The power of His grace has granted me freedom, and I am not condemned. I have acceptance in Christ Jesus. The power of the spirit of life in Christ has set me free from the law of sin and death. I have been set free to serve Him without fear all the days of my life. I have the spirit of power, the spirit of love, and a sound mind. I bask in His love; I am fulfilled in His love. I partake of the divine nature; I am washed in the blood of the eternal covenant, redeemed, eternally saved, and justified by faith. I am adopted by God into the household of faith; I am a son, and He is my Father. I am provided for according to the abundance of His love, and I lack nothing. I am confident in the love of my savior for me. The undying love of my God is my covering in the day of trouble; the boundless love of the Lord breaks the bond of death and the grave. I have the life of the Son of God and the fullness of the Holy Spirit. I abound in all that represents a need. Heaven answers to me, and the earth responds to me. I walk in divine health. I go from strength to strength; I walk in the blessing of Zion. I experience the power of Gods favor daily. I will not be denied, and nothing can separate me from the love of God. I am blessed. I am a blessing to all I encounter. My life is an addition of value to creation.

In Jesuss name, I believe and say amen.

Selected Affirmations

I have been set free to serve Him without fear all the days of my life. I have the spirit of power, the spirit of love, and a sound mind.

The undying love of my God is my covering in the day of trouble; the boundless love of the Lord breaks the bond of death and the grave. I have the life of the Son of God and the fullness of the Holy Spirit. I abound in all that represents a need.

Suggested Scriptures

Who hath delivered us from the power of darkness, and hath translated us into the kingdom of his dear Son. (Colossians 1:13)

But I will sing of thy power; yea, I will sing aloud of thy mercy in the morning: for thou hast been my defence and refuge in the day of my trouble. (Psalm 59:16)

Labour not for the meat which perisheth, but for that meat which endureth unto everlasting life, which the Son of man shall give unto you: for him hath God the Father sealed. (John 6:27)

Now the God of hope fill you with all joy and peace in believing, that ye may abound in hope, through the power of the Holy Ghost. (Romans 15:13)

21. Perfected in His Love

Today, I speak over my life and my household that God will amaze us with pleasant surprises and vindicate our cause.

I am seated in heavenly places in Christ Jesus, far above principalities, powers, and wicked spirits. I cannot be touched, for He has given His word concerning me, and no harm shall befall me. I walk under the power of the divine covenant; God is eternally committed to me. I am the recipient of Gods faithfulness; no carefully designed conspiracy of hell against my God-ordained destiny shall stand. There is no enchantment against me, and there is no divination against me, for I am above and established in God. My covenant promises are intact. God sees me through. I am delivered from every insurrection of the enemy; God fights my battles, and I have the victory. I am stronger than my adversaries, and I have been strengthened with the spirit of might in my inward man. No man can stand before me. I am secure in God. Nothing makes me afraid. Fear is defeated in my life. The Lord is my light and my salvation; there is nothing to fear. My life and times are in His hands, I am loved perfectly and perfected in love, and He lifts my head. I am elevated and promoted, angels watch over my every step to keep me from falling, and the blood speaks mercy on my behalf. I am consistently progressive and progressively consistent. God is the force of my life. He rejoices over me with singing, and my hands are lifted in triumph over my enemies. I am above always and never beneath; I have unprecedented favor and grace so amazing.

In Jesuss name, I believe and say amen.

SELECTED AFFIRMATIONS

The Lord is my light and my salvation; there is nothing to fear. My life and times are in His hands. I am loved perfectly and perfected in love.

No carefully designed conspiracy of hell against my God-ordained destiny shall stand.

SUGGESTED SCRIPTURES

The LORD is my light and my salvation; whom shall I fear? the LORD is the strength of my life; of whom shall I be afraid? (Psalm 27:1)

Behold, I have graven thee upon the palms of my hands; thy walls are continually before me. (Isaiah 49:16)

Surely there is no enchantment against Jacob, neither is there any divination against Israel: according to this time it shall be said of Jacob and of Israel, What hath God wrought! (Numbers 23:23)

There shall no evil befall thee, neither shall any plague come nigh thy dwelling. (Psalm 91:10)

22. Walking in the Light

Today, I speak over my life and my household that God leads us through every season and that our steps are ordered by the Lord.

I am righteous before the Lord. My path shines brighter, like a shiny light toward a perfect day. Darkness cannot comprehend the brightness of the light of my life. I blaze forth as the glory of the Lord. My time has come; its my turn, and nothing can stop the illumination of my life and time. With the brightness of the light of Gods word the world will see my light, and my generation will experience the radiance of the glory of God in my life. Darkness departs, and the light of God blazes through. The glory of the Lord is risen upon me. I arise and shine. Kings come to the brightness of my rising, and princes find their way through. I will not walk in darkness. The son of the stranger shall be my vine dresser. I am exalted in the light and in the view of all; my lifting is undeniable, and there is no controversy about my promotion. Many shall entreat my favor, for I am the called of the Lord. I am chosen, elected, and selected for favor; I step toward greatness, and I am embraced by great success. The lines are fallen for me in pleasant places. I possess the secret riches of hidden places; supernatural grace of everlasting abundance is converted to me. The mighty in the land submit themselves to me, and I instruct the elders at the gate. I am established in the light of the countenance of my King. Nothing brings me down, for I occupy my place in the scheme of things, and I rule in the midst of my enemies. The brightness of my light will not grow dim. I am stronger than my foes. I am the blessed of God.

In Jesuss name, I believe and say amen.

Selected Affirmations

My path shines brighter, like a shiny light toward a perfect day. Darkness cannot comprehend the brightness of the light of my life.

I am established in the light of the countenance of my King. Nothing brings me down; the brightness of my light will not grow dim.

Suggested Scriptures

And the light shineth in darkness; and the darkness comprehended it not. (John 1:5)

And the Gentiles shall come to thy light, and kings to the brightness of thy rising. (Isaiah 60:3)

They shall come with weeping, and with supplications will I lead them: I will cause them to walk by the rivers of waters in a straight way, wherein they shall not stumble: for I am a father to Israel, and Ephraim is my firstborn. (Jeremiah 31:9)

The lines are fallen unto me in pleasant places; yea, I have a goodly heritage. (Psalm 16:6)

23. Saved and Sanctified

Today, I speak over my life and my household that we enjoy the full benefits of salvation and that the power of the Almighty makes the blessing of redemption a reality in our experience.

My sins are forgiven; I have received mercy from the God of all the earth. I am not condemned, for I am accepted in the beloved and live by the power of the spirit of life in Christ Jesus. I am healed, and I live in divine health. His body was broken so mine is made whole in Him. I am the righteousness of God in Christ Jesus. My steps are ordered into the fullness of Gods blessing; I have divine assistance and angelic support. I am protected, and the hedge around me is secure. Whatever I lay my hands on prospers. I have peace with God, and my ways are pleasing unto my God. I am a person of faith, and I believe the word of God. My enemies are at peace with me. I have a living hope and certain future; all things work together for my good. I am called according to purpose. I will fulfill my God-ordained destiny. I am saved and sanctified; I have the power of the Holy Spirit in me. I partake of the divine nature. I am a regent of God on earth. I am a prince that has power with God; the breath of God is in me. I walk in dominion, and I am blessed with every blessing in the heavenly places in Christ Jesus. God rules in my life, and I am perfectly placed in the will of God. I lack nothing, for I am provided for by God, and He is my source. My mouth is satisfied with good things. I eat the good of the land. I have the support of heaven; I have the oil of gladness and ease.

In Jesuss name, I believe and say amen.

Selected Affirmations

My sins are forgiven, I have received mercy from the God of all the earth, and I am not condemned.

My steps are ordered into the fullness of Gods blessing; I am perfectly placed in the will of God.

Suggested Scriptures

And when he saw their faith, he said unto him, Man, thy sins are forgiven thee. (Luke 5:20)

The steps of a good man are ordered by the LORD: and he delighteth in his way. (Psalm 37:23)

The elders which are among you I exhort, who am also an elder, and a witness of the sufferings of Christ, and also a partaker of the gl (1 Peter 5:1)

For by one offering he hath perfected forever them that are sanctified. (Hebrews 10:14)

24. The Enabler

Today, I speak over my life and my household the peace of God that passes all understanding and the power of His mercy, love, and favor.

God comes through for me in all things on all fronts, at all sides. God fights for me, so I cant lose. I am a winner and victorious. I am a believer, so nothing is impossible for me; the power that created the heavens and the earth is at work in me. God loves me perfectly; He is my light and my salvation. He is the force that guards my life, and I do not fear. I am strong in the Lord and in the power of His might. The word of the Lord works wonders in my life. I encounter the miraculous workings of His power daily. Life is meaningful for me; I have destiny in full view. My goals come through, the Lord enables me, and I can do all things through Christ, who strengthens me. I am saved to serve the Lord my God without fear. My service is not in vain. I have the full benefits of redemption. Heavens resources are at my disposal, for I am a covenant child. My promotion is constant, and my lifting is consistent; my promises are real, and God is committed to me by love. His blood bears witness that I am the righteous. I drink from the streams of rejoicing; the enemy has no say in my life. My story ends in glory. God is my shield, fortress, and strong tower. I am totally defended and completely protected. My inheritance is in place. I am the recipient of Gods amazing grace. These are the times of my showings and the period of my vindication. God validates my calling with supernatural breakthroughs. I am the beloved of my Father. I have great success. I am a blessing to my generation and an inspiration to the next. Global prominence is a possibility for me.

In Jesuss name, I believe and say amen.

Selected Affirmations

The word of the Lord works wonders in my life. I encounter the miraculous workings of His power daily. Life is meaningful for me, and I have destiny in full view.

Suggested Scriptures

So mightily grew the word of God and prevailed. (Acts 19:20)

This book of the law shall not depart out of thy mouth; but thou shalt meditate therein day and night, that thou mayest observe to do according to all that is written therein: for then thou shalt make thy way prosperous, and then thou shalt have good success. (Joshua 1:8)

The LORD is my rock, and my fortress, and my deliverer; my God, my strength, in whom I will trust; my buckler, and the horn of my salvation, and my high tower. (Psalm 18:2)

And to Jesus the mediator of the new covenant, and to the blood of sprinkling, that speaketh better things than that of Abel. (Hebrews 12:24)

25. Sealed by His Spirit

Today, I speak over my life and my household that God is the strength of our lives and that He is our portion forever.

I am protected eternally under the shadow of His wings, I am kept secure in the hollow of His palm, and no harm shall befall me. No evil shall come near my dwelling, for I am constantly watched over by an innumerable company of angels. I excel in all I do because God is my helper; the maker of heaven and earth has me in His sight. The God that keeps me neither slumbers nor sleeps; I rest assured that I am completely covered in the love of my savior. The sun shall not smite me by day; the moon will not smite me by night. My soul is preserved, and I walk in divine health, for I am sealed by the precious Holy Spirit. My future is bright, my past is buried, my sins are forgiven, and the curse of the law is reversed. I am saved. I am delivered. I am sanctified. I have been justified, my shame is turned into glory, my life is precious in His eyes, and I am jealously kept as the apple of His eye. I enter into a season of divine restoration. Goodness and mercy chase, pursue, find, and follow me; I am favored wherever I turn. I am honored by men, and kings and royalty entreat my favor. I am numbered with the strong and take my place among the mighty in the land. He has extended my coasts. My borders have been expanded. I dwell in the land of limitless possibilities. My destiny is sure. I walk in light, and nothing frustrates me. My story has changed. I receive His faithfulness daily. I am born to reign, and I rule in life. Wisdom distinguishes me. I stand out from the crowd. Of the brightness of my rising, there is no end. I am led by the spirit. I am a son of God. I am blessed above the rest.

In Jesuss name, I believe and say amen.

Selected Affirmations

The God that keeps me neither slumbers nor sleeps; I rest assured that I am completely covered in the love of my Savior.

I am sealed by the precious Holy Spirit; my future is bright, my past is buried, my sins are forgiven, and the curse of the law is reversed.

Suggested Scriptures

Behold, he that keepeth Israel shall neither slumber nor sleep. (Psalm 121:4)

In whom ye also trusted, after that ye heard the word of truth, the gospel of your salvation: in whom also after that ye believed, ye were sealed with that holy Spirit of promise. (Ephesians 1:13)

Therefore we are buried with him by baptism into death: that like as Christ was raised up from the dead by the glory of the Father, even so we also should walk in newness of life. (Romans 6:4)

I write unto you, little children, because your sins are forgiven you for his names sake. (1 John 2:12)

26. Gloriously Recreated

Today, I speak over my life and my household that our season of drought is over.

I step into the unending season of abundance of rain. I make a successful transition from being a survivor to being an overcomer. I move from desperation to declaration of the positive power of Gods word. My world is recreated gloriously. The word of God is fulfilled in all the areas of my life, and I have received sure mercies of David. I receive the favor, blessings, renewed hope, and amazing grace of God. I have solace in times of trial and comfort in times of pain. God is my peace in the eye of the perfect storm. Unmerited favor is mine; even though I am undeserving, I receive it. I am redeemed from my past, present, and future wrongs. My broken dreams have life again; I shine brightly in the light of His eternal freedom. Every wall of separation is broken down, and I have unfettered access to the presence of the glorious King. All things have become new to me. The power that keeps the heavens keeps me. I am a fruitful bough whose branches reach over the wall; I am established from sea to sea. I walk in dominion, and I do not lose ground. I am strong in the Lord and in the power of His might. The winds blow in all that is mine; my storehouses are full of Gods bounties, and my harvest is plentiful, rich in goodness. My year is crowned with plenty, and my life is a testimony of Gods goodness. My mouth is filled with good things, my lips sing the praise, I experience a raise, and my profile is on the rise. As I go forward my growth is unhindered. The shackles are broken, and I am emancipated. I activate the will of the Father. I prosper, I am in health, and I am unstoppable. I am born of God. I overcome the world. I am immune to failure; success is attracted to me. I have great success. I am the blessed of God.

In Jesuss name, I believe and say amen.

Selected Affirmations

I am redeemed from my past, present, and future wrongs. My broken dreams have life again.

I have solace in times of trial and comfort in times of pain. God is my peace in the eye of the perfect storm.

Suggested Scriptures

The beast of the field shall honour me, the dragons and the owls: because I give waters in the wilderness, and rivers in the desert, to give drink to my people, my chosen. (Isaiah 43:20)

Incline your ear, and come unto me: hear, and your soul shall live; and I will make an everlasting covenant with you, even the sure mercies of David. (Isaiah 55:3)

This is my comfort in my affliction: for thy word hath quickened me. (Psalm 119:50)

Behold, I will do a new thing; now it shall spring forth; shall ye not know it? I will even make a way in the wilderness, and rivers in the desert. (Isaiah 43:19)

27. Surrendered to His Will

Today, I speak over my life and my household that God increases us in every way and upholds us with the righteousness of His right hand.

I yield and surrender to His will, and I take advantage of the fullness of His power. I am healed. I am restored. There is no loss of any kind. I walk in the safety accorded me by the wisdom of God. I am fruitful as the Lord has commanded. The curse is reversed. I am the delight of the Father. Heaven hears when I call, and the earth responds when I speak. I have the authority to trample on snakes and scorpions and to overcome all the power of the enemy; nothing will hurt me. Kings are rebuked for me. Angels have charge over me. The hedge of protection around me is still in place. I am hidden in Christ and in God. I am delivered. My past is past. My future is secure. My present is full of goodness. I am a winner, and I have the power to make a change. I dwell in light. Darkness cannot withstand me. I enter into a season of ceaseless increase on every side. I am comforted by the spirit of God. I move into the fullness of Gods promise for my life. My God fights my battles, and I am victorious in His name. I am protected; I am kept as the apple of His eye. He is my shepherd. I am led into abundance. I am taught to profit. I have nothing missing and nothing broken. My cause is not lost. My dreams are not dead. I am a blessing to my generation and generations yet unborn. The word of God works for me. The heavens are opened to me, and God assists me. My helpers find me. The earth supports me. I live in the sufficient and amazing grace of God. I am a recipient of His mercy.

In Jesuss name, I believe and say amen.

Selected Affirmations

My past is past. My future is secure. My present is full of goodness.

I am fruitful as the Lord has commanded.

Heaven hears when I call, and the earth responds when I speak. I have the authority to trample on snakes and scorpions and to overcome all the power of the enemy; nothing will hurt me.

Suggested Scriptures

And he increased his people greatly; and made them stronger than their enemies. (Psalm 105:24)

Saying, Father, if thou be willing, remove this cup from me: nevertheless not my will, but thine, be done. (Luke 22:42)

Christ hath redeemed us from the curse of the law, being made a curse for us: for it is written, Cursed is every one that hangeth on a tree. (Galatians 3:13)

Behold, I give unto you power to tread on serpents and scorpions, and over all the power of the enemy: and nothing shall by any means hurt you. (Luke 10:19)

28. Loaded with Power

Today, I speak over my life and my household that we will increase in the revelation of our God and that the Most High will take us to new heights in Him.

I bask in the goodness of Gods glory. The dew of heaven refreshes me. Power flows from me to change situations and circumstances around me. I step into the epicenter of Gods divine plan for my life. It is my turn, and its my time. My change has come. Nothing can stop me; I move into an era of limitless possibilities, and I am totally liberated to operate in power. I see increase; I have the scepter of unlimited authority, my rod buds, and I am distinguished amongst my peers. My case is different, for my story has changed. My walk leads me to greatness. My destiny is intact. I cannot be stranded, for God is eternally on my side. I see my way through to the top. I am the zenith of Gods creation, formed in love, loaded with power, justified by faith, and saved by grace that is destined by heaven and earthly relevant. I am a child of promise, a son of consolation. I am immune to failure and attracted to success; nothing stands between me and greatness. Im a believer, and my path is flooded with light. I prevail in every situation of life. I am strong in the Lord and in the power of His might. My faith is good for the fight; I have great faith, and my faith will not fail. God covers my head in the midst of battle. I am victorious.

In Jesuss name, I believe and say amen.

Selected Affirmations

Power flows from me to change situations and circumstances around me.

I am totally liberated to operate in power.

Suggested Scriptures

Then shalt thou delight thyself in the Lord; and I will cause thee to ride upon the high places of the earth, and feed thee with the heritage of Jacob thy father: for the mouth of the Lord hath spoken it. (Isaiah 58:14)

For the seed shall be prosperous; the vine shall give her fruit, and the ground shall give her increase, and the heavens shall give their dew; and I will cause the remnant of this people to possess all these things. (Zechariah 8:12)

And it came to pass, that on the morrow Moses went into the tabernacle of witness; and, behold, the rod of Aaron for the house of Levi was budded, and brought forth buds, and bloomed blossoms, and yielded almonds. (Numbers 17:8)

Now unto him that is able to do exceeding abundantly above all that we ask or think, according to the power that worketh in us. (Ephesians 3:20)

29. Distinguished by His Love

Today, I speak over my life and my household that God remembers us for good.

I am forgiven and never forsaken; Gods love distinguishes me for divine assistance. I have favor with God and with men. The Father upholds me and lifts me above the trouble and decay of the world. I am sanctified and set apart unto righteousness. The fountains of the deep are broken for me, and the drought is over. I hear, see, and experience the sound of the abundance of rain. Dryness is turned around, and I walk in the refreshing pleasure of the dew of heaven. I see the manifestation of the glory of God; I will not miss my season of visitation of the spirit of God. I encounter God afresh, and I have received mercy, goodness, favor, peace, comfort on all sides, and joy unspeakable full of glory. The siege is over; the power of the enemy is broken, and today is the day of salvation. Life gives birth to life eternal, life abundance, and the fullness of life. I walk unhindered in His presence, and I have the fullness of joy. I have the pleasure of His household forever more. My mountain stands strong, my life matters, and the top of my high places are visible to the eyes. My future is settled in God, I am graced for global prominence, my seed endures, and my strides are giant. As I go forward, I get more than I bargained for. The throne is prepared for me, and I walk in my three-fold anointing. I am a kingly priest and a prophet to my generation. The sons of the stranger will serve me. I am secure in God. My destiny cannot be derailed.

In Jesuss name, I believe and say amen.

Selected Affirmations

Gods love distinguishes me for divine assistance; I have favor with God and with men.

I am sanctified and set apart unto righteousness. The fountains of the deep are broken for me; the drought is over. I hear, see, and experience the sound of the abundance of rain.

Suggested Scriptures

And Elijah said unto Ahab, Get thee up, eat and drink; for there is a sound of abundance of rain. (1 Kings 18:41)

Then they that feared the Lord spake often one to another: and the Lord hearkened, and heard it, and a book of remembrance was written before him for them that feared the Lord, and that thought upon his name. (Malachi 3:16)

And the angel said unto her, Fear not, Mary: for thou hast found favour with God. (Luke 1:30)

And the Lord visited Sarah as he had said, and the Lord did unto Sarah as he had spoken. (Genesis 21:1)

30. Directed by His Spirit

Today, I speak over my life and my household that God hears us when we call.

I hear when He calls, and I am delivered from every distraction and from destruction. God hastens to my help; I am angel assisted and spirit directed; I see and jump over every pit dug for my footsteps. I will not be caught by any net set to ensnare me. My life is precious, and God leads and protects me always. I am anointed to conquer the hell gates; I am battle ready, and my victory is assured. God is my pillar of strength, my righteous banner. The burden is lifted, and the yoke is shattered; every heavy basket is taken off my shoulders. I am marked for honor. I have survived the flood and the fire; I come out purified like burnished gold. My destiny emerges gloriously, and I am sought after for favor and honor. My light shines forth to the ends of the earth. I am elevated by grace for glory. The works of my hands are sanctified. I am Christs workmanship unto good works. God loves me, and God has justified me by faith. I am selected by the Holy Spirit for promotion in this season; I am set aside for distinction. I am called according to Gods purpose, and my life will not end in shame; my future is painted in glorious colors. I manifest Gods power and loving kindness. I am filled with the power of the holy spirit of God. I am a child born in season; my day is here, and my future starts now. I grow in wisdom, grace, glory, and the peace of God. My life is a testimony of Gods faithfulness. I am a living witness of Gods divine providence, for God rescues me. I am not stranded in life. I have the light of His countenance. I am perfected in His love.

In Jesuss name, I believe and say amen.

Selected Affirmations

I am delivered from every distraction and from destruction; God hastens to my help. I am angel assisted and spirit directed.

I am filled with the power of the holy spirit of God.

Suggested Scriptures

And it shall come to pass, that before they call, I will answer; and while they are yet speaking, I will hear. (Isaiah 65:24)

Our soul is escaped as a bird out of the snare of the fowlers: the snare is broken, and we are escaped. (Psalm 124:7)

Now thanks be unto God, which always causeth us to triumph in Christ, and maketh manifest the savour of his knowledge by us in every place. (2 Corinthians 2:14)

For we are his workmanship, created in Christ Jesus unto good works, which God hath before ordained that we should walk in them. (Ephesians 2:10)

31. It's a New Season

Today, I speak over my life and my household that God has changed our story and given us a new chance at life.

I have a new start. I have help divine; I have assistance from on high. I am not alone, for I am supported by an innumerable company of angels. The earth is ready for my elevation, and this generation awaits the announcement of my promotion. I see change for the better; I see increase all around me. As I step into my new season, God walks with me, so nothing makes me afraid. I have the grace to live free of every hold of the enemy; the chains of limitation are broken. I sit at the table prepared for me. I walk in greatness, and God favors me. I walk in righteousness, and He is my sanctification. I have access into His divine presence; I am accepted in the beloved, and I have been comforted on all sides, for God has delivered me. I am healed, and I live in health; I live above strain, stress, and sin. I have been forgiven; my past is forgotten. I have the power, I am willing and obedient, and I eat the good of the land. My mouth is filled with plenty. God orders my steps, and I walk into the realms of possibilities; I am established in success. Nothing is difficult or impossible for me.

In Jesuss name, I believe and say amen.

Selected Affirmations

God has delivered me. I am healed, and I live in health. I live above strain, stress, and sin. I have been forgiven; my past is forgotten.

Suggested Scriptures

Now also when I am old and grey headed, O God, forsake me not; until I have shewed thy strength unto this generation, and thy power to every one that is to come. (Psalm 71:18)

Therefore sprang there even of one, and him as good as dead, so many as the stars of the sky in multitude, and as the sand which is by the sea shore innumerable. (Hebrews 11:12)

And, behold, the angel of the Lord came upon him, and a light shined in the prison: and he smote Peter on the side, and raised him up, saying, Arise up quickly. And his chains fell off from his hands. (Acts 12:7)

Thou shalt increase my greatness, and comfort me on every side. (Psalm 71:21)

32. Safe in the Hands of God

Today, I speak over my life and my household that God will amaze us with the manifestation of His goodness and surprise us with favor everywhere we turn.

I will see the hand of God in every situation; my interest is protected, and I am prepared for divine appointment. My change is now. God has answered my prayers according to the righteousness of His hand; my posterity is secured. God has rewarded me according to His graciousness, and I am protected by His pleasure. The gates of brass are broken, the bars of iron are shattered, and He has brought me into a new estate in life. My story has been rewritten; from today as I go forward I grow from faith to faith, and I grow in wisdom. The spirit of God is made manifest in me; I am led into the fullness of Gods divine program for my destiny, Nothing is difficult to achieve, for I am enlightened by the power of His victorious right hand; I receive the enabling power of the Almighty to work with ease through the seemingly difficult places of the earth. Every effort of mine yields maximum result; I have hope restored, and my harvest is full. I am justified in love and commended by faith. I am not condemned, for I am led by the power of righteousness for the sake of the saviors love. I am forgiven and not forsaken; I am delivered and not marked for destruction. I am a wonder unto many, for God is pleased with me; my enemies are at peace with me, and my opponents withdraw in awe of Gods presence in my life. I have the victory. I am a winner.

In Jesuss name, I believe and say amen.

Selected Affirmations

God has answered my prayers according to the righteousness of His hand.

I grow from faith to faith, I grow in wisdom, and the spirit of God is made manifest in me. I am led into the fullness of Gods divine program for my destiny.

Suggested Scriptures

Blessed is the man whom thou choosest, and causest to approach unto thee, that he may dwell in thy courts: we shall be satisfied with the goodness of thy house, even of thy holy temple. (Psalm 65:4)

I will go before thee, and make the crooked places straight: I will break in pieces the gates of brass, and cut in sunder the bars of iron. (Isaiah 45:2)

There is therefore now no condemnation to them which are in Christ Jesus, who walk not after the flesh, but after the Spirit. (Romans 8:1)

Let your conversation be without covetousness; and be content with such things as ye have: for he hath said, I will never leave thee, nor forsake thee. (Hebrews 13:5)

33. Born on Purpose

Today, I speak over my life and my household that God has saved and delivered us from shame, disgrace, and destruction.

His eternal love sanctifies me and sets me aside for destinys sake. My purpose is attainable, and I am established completely in His will. I work toward perfection, and nothing hinders me from becoming the very best in God. I am kept jealousy as the apple of His eye, the hedge of protection around me is maintained, and the angels have charge over me. As I am led by the spirit into all truth, the light of the countenance of the Lord goes before me. I skip over every pit, I leap over every wall, I run through a troop, and I run into the tower that is the name of the Lord. I find safety under the tabernacle of His wings. Heaven protects my posterity, and my heritage is preserved. I am the beloved of the Lord, and He keeps me on the paths of righteousness for His names sake. I suffer no loss; I am assisted in all things at all times. I am not forgotten, and I am not forsaken. My faith keeps me, and I walk in the miraculous on a daily basis. I am strong for the fight, I am victorious in battle, my head is covered, and I am shielded from every arrow of destruction. Every conspiracy is destroyed; every accusation is refuted. I move freely into the prepared place. I have received grace for grace, and the curse is reversed. My life blossoms. Strength is renewed. I walk into my season of restoration and refreshing. I am a recipient of His mercy.

In Jesuss name, I believe and say amen.

Selected Affirmations

I find safety under the tabernacle of His wings. Heaven protects my posterity; my heritage is preserved.

His eternal love sanctifies me and sets me aside for destinys sake. My purpose is attainable, and I am established completely in His will.

Suggested Scriptures

For your shame ye shall have double; and for confusion they shall rejoice in their portion: therefore in their land they shall possess the double: everlasting joy shall be unto them. (Isaiah 61:7)

Before I formed thee in the belly I knew thee; and before thou camest forth out of the womb I sanctified thee, and I ordained thee a prophet unto the nations. (Jeremiah 1:5)

For thus saith the Lord of hosts; After the glory hath he sent me unto the nations which spoiled you: for he that toucheth you toucheth the apple of his eye. (Zechariah 2:8)

For by thee I have run through a troop: by my God have I leaped over a wall. (2 Samuel 22:30)

34. My Divine Heritage

Today, I speak over my life and my household that God will enlarge our coasts and extend our territories.

I conquer new frontiers and break new grounds in all areas of my endeavors, and I access fresh revelation of the Almighty for elevation. I have inspiration; I enjoy more divine redirection for maximum manifestation. I am a source of impact for my days on earth, and generations yet unborn will celebrate my contribution. I am not a waste but an addition to value. I am relevant on earth and approved by heaven. I fulfill all that is written of me in the volume of the books, and the will of God is done in my life. I suffer no loss, and Gods grace flows freely toward me. I am profiled for greatness; I am a city set on a hill. My light cannot be hidden; I am a beacon of hope to all around me. I stand strong in victory, and no evil comes near me, for I am protected by the power in the blood of the eternal covenant. Everything becomes new around me. Strangers give up their territories in dread and fear, I walk freely through the land, and I claim my divine inheritance. I receive the hidden riches of secret places. I activate the Fathers will, and I receive a worthy inheritance. It is secured in the name of the Lord my God. I walk in the rights and privileges of my heavenly citizenship. I cannot be denied, and I am not delayed. All things happen for me in His time. My heritage is divine.

In Jesuss name, I believe and say amen.

Selected Affirmations

I conquer new frontiers and break new grounds in all areas of my endeavors; I access fresh revelation of the Almighty for elevation.

Suggested Scriptures

And Jabez called on the God of Israel, saying, Oh that thou wouldest bless me indeed, and enlarge my coast, and that thine hand might be with me, and that thou wouldest keep me from evil, that it may not grieve me! And God granted him that which he requested. (1 Chronicles 4:10)

That the God of our Lord Jesus Christ, the Father of glory, may give unto you the spirit of wisdom and revelation in the knowledge of him. (Ephesians 1:17)

Then said I, Lo, I come (in the volume of the book it is written of me,) to do thy will, O God. (Hebrews 10:7)

Ye are the light of the world. A city that is set on an hill cannot be hid. (Matthew 5:14)

35. Established in His Covenant

Today, I speak over my life and my household that Gods amazing grace flows freely to us.

God stands for me in every situation and circumstance; I am not alone, and I am not on my own. I am distinguished by the ever-abiding presence of the Lord. Where the law has failed, the grace of God has prevailed. I am forgiven and not forsaken, for the love of God preserves me, and the power of the spirit keeps me. Favor from the Father finds me. I am a prince with power, and I am blessed with every spiritual blessing in heaven in Christ Jesus. I am numbered amongst the blessed on earth, for I am a partaker of the Abrahamic covenant. The curse of the law is reversed; I have the generation-spanning blessing of God the Father in Christ Jesus. The force of redemption selects me for the marvelous touch of the Holy Ghost. I exceed all expectations, and I excel in all my hands find to do. I am a source of comfort. I am a part of the solution to the ills of this generation, and I am rich in wisdom. I am a man of peace, I walk in health, I have great faith, and I walk in the light. I will not stumble, I will not fail, and I will not fall. I am a sign and a wonder to many. God is at work in me; I do His pleasure, and my ways are pleasing unto God. I am covered by the blood of the eternal covenant. I abide in safety, for the Lord is my refuge and fortress. Fear is defeated. God is the strength of my life; I am protected, and my future is secure. Grace validates my place and position in Christ Jesus, and nothing can unseat me. No one can separate me from the love of God. I live above the constraints of the world. My ways and paths are lined with divine possibilities and potentials. I have overcome failure, shame, and disgrace. I am next in line for the manifestation of Gods supernatural elevation. All eyes will see the revelation of Gods glory in my life. I am the blessed of God.

In Jesuss name, I believe and say amen.

Selected Affirmations

The force of redemption selects me for the marvelous touch of the Holy Ghost.

I live above the constraints of the world. My ways and paths are lined with divine possibilities and potentials.

I have overcome failure, shame, and disgrace.

Suggested Scriptures

And God is able to make all grace abound toward you; that ye, always having all sufficiency in all things, may abound to every good work. (2 Corinthians 9:8)

And I will pray the Father, and he shall give you another Comforter, that he may abide with you for ever. (John 14:16)

Blessed be the God and Father of our Lord Jesus Christ, who hath blessed us with all spiritual blessings in heavenly places in Christ. (Ephesians 1:3)

They shall come with weeping, and with supplications will I lead them: I will cause them to walk by the rivers of waters in a straight way, wherein they shall not stumble: for I am a father to Israel, and Ephraim is my firstborn. (Jeremiah 31:9)

36. The Spirit of Wisdom

Today, I speak over my life and my household that God is our source and our sustenance.

I am not stranded, nor am I lost in confusion; the light of His countenance illuminates my path, and darkness is as light before me. My eyes behold the sun, and I experience the goodness of the Father afresh. My heart finds rest in God alone. My bones are revived; I have the breath of the spirit of God inside me. I stand tall in the midst of every challenge, and I overcome by the power of the spirit. Might and dominion find expression in my life; I am distinguished and set apart for the victorious life. Problems, situations, and circumstances bow to the workings of the spirit of divine wisdom in my life. I stand out in the crowd: I am wiser than my peers, I have more wisdom than the aged, and I am more endowed than my teachers. I am a source of reference and a solution provider. The earth responds to me, and heaven answers when I call. Nothing is beyond the grace of God on my life; I can do all things through Christ, who strengthens me. I am prepared for greatness. I am sustained in health and suffer no loss, for I am covered by the power in the name and the blood of the eternal covenant. God holds me by the strength of His right hand. He watches over me, and His angels have charge over me; I am divinely helped and heavenly assisted. I live in the sufficient and amazing grace of God. I am a recipient of His mercy. I prosper, I am in health, and I am unstoppable. I am born of God. I overcome the world. I am immune to failure, and success is attracted to me. I have great success. I am the blessed of God.

In Jesuss name, I believe and say amen.

Selected Affirmations

I have the breath of the spirit of God inside me. I stand tall in the midst of every challenge; I overcome by the power of the spirit.

Suggested Scriptures

Thy word is a lamp unto my feet, and a light unto my path. (Psalm 119:105)

And if thou draw out thy soul to the hungry, and satisfy the afflicted soul; then shall thy light rise in obscurity, and thy darkness be as the noon day. (Isaiah 58:10)

And it shall come to pass in that day, I will hear, saith the Lord, I will hear the heavens, and they shall hear the earth. (Hosea 2:21)

I have more understanding than all my teachers: for thy testimonies are my meditation. (Psalm 119:99)

37. Set to Reign

Today, I speak over my life and my household that God is for us and that the Almighty is on our side.

I will not see shame, nor will I be disgraced. I awake to mercy and arise to the favor of the living God. Everything that concerns me receives the approval of the God of all creation. My destiny is divinely supported and assisted. God is my keeper and my shield; I am protected, and no evil comes near me. I walk in the light of His word, so my path is illuminated. My expectations are not truncated, and I fulfill my purpose. My confidence is in the Lord; He is my fortress. I will not be shaken, for my heart dwells in safety. His faithfulness abides. God leads me by the hand, and I am delivered safely into the realms of fulfillment. My struggles are over, and I see my way clear into the era of validation. I am set and prepared to reign in life; nothing stands between me and greatness, for I am the righteousness of God in Christ Jesus. I emerge as a miracle and sign to my generation. I abide in strength; I am surrounded with favor as a shield and am guarded by an innumerable company of angels. I am born of God, and I have overcome the world. I have great faith in the grace of my God. Nations bow at my feet. My helpers find me. My sins are forgiven, my wait is over, and my season of divine visitation is here. It is my appointed time. I step into my season of rest and restoration; my blessings come from every wing of the wind. I am entitled to a lift. I am primed for promotion, and I activate the Fathers will for my life. Every good and perfect gift from the Father is mine. My dreams come true, and my hope is secure.

In Jesuss name, I believe and say amen.

Selected Affirmations

I am set and prepared to reign in life; nothing stands between me and greatness.

Everything that concerns me receives the approval of the God of all creation.

Suggested Scriptures

Though an host should encamp against me, my heart shall not fear: though war should rise against me, in this will I be confident. (Psalm 27:3)

For if by one mans offence death reigned by one; much more they which receive abundance of grace and of the gift of righteousness shall reign in life by one, Jesus Christ. (Romans 5:17)

For he hath made him to be sin for us, who knew no sin; that we might be made the righteousness of God in him. (2 Corinthians 5:21)

And kings shall be thy nursing fathers, and their queens thy nursing mothers: they shall bow down to thee with their face toward the earth, and lick up the dust of thy feet; and thou shalt know that I am the Lord: for they shall not be ashamed that wait for me. (Isaiah 49:23)

38. It's My Due Season

Today, I speak over my life and my household that its our due season; the long wait is over.

God comes through for me, and the change appointed to me has come. I emerge a force to be reckoned with, a great voice with an undeniable destiny; my purpose cannot be missed. I am jet-propelled into the fullness of Gods preordained place of divine fulfillment. Doors of opportunity open up for me, and I find expression for my gifts and calling. It is my season; everything works in my favor. I receive strength from aboveI have the inspiration of the Holy Spirit. I move into position; I take my place. Opposition melts into insignificance before me. I enter into the newness of Gods revealed plan for eternal establishment for my life. I mount with wings like the eagle. My feet finds the rock, which have been delivered from the sinking sand. The fountains of the deep are broken, and the heavens give their rain. Its a change for the better, for the drought is over. I have the former and the latter rain at the same time. It is my bountiful harvest time. The days of my appointment are here; it is my due date. Promises are fulfilled, debts are cancelled, and grace is poured out. God is glorified. Its a new season all over again, and I have a fresh start. Its my turn because its my time. My joy is ceaseless, my praise unstoppable. My victory is endless.

In Jesuss name, I believe and say amen.

Selected Affirmations

Doors of opportunity open up for me, and I find expression for my gifts and calling. It is my season; everything works in my favor.

Suggested Scriptures

That I will give you the rain of your land in his due season, the first rain and the latter rain, that thou mayest gather in thy corn, and thy wine, and thine oil. (Deuteronomy 11:14)

But the angel of the Lord by night opened the prison doors, and brought them forth, and said. (Acts 5:19)

But they that wait upon the Lord shall renew their strength; they shall mount up with wings as eagles; they shall run, and not be weary; and they shall walk, and not faint. (Isaiah 40:31)

In the six hundredth year of Noahs life, in the second month, the seventeenth day of the month, the same day were all the fountains of the great deep broken up, and the windows of heaven were opened. (Genesis 7:11)

39. Preserved to Prosper

Today, I speak over my life and my household that Gods love secures a great future for us and comforts us through every situation of life.

Though I walk through the valley of the shadow of death, no evil comes near me, for God is with me. His presence is my shield, and fear is destroyed by the power of His love. I rest in the knowledge of His loving kindness and am not moved by the sudden destruction of the wicked. I am protected from every devastation and shielded from fear. The enemy near me is totally powerless. I am protected, for I am hidden in the hollow of the hand of the Almighty. Nothing makes me afraid. I have found my peace in the shadow of His wings, and I drink from the streams of rejoicing. My God is my King. He is my Lord and my Father. I have an eternally enduring heritage. I am kept and jealously guarded as the apple of His eye. My life is precious to Him. He gives men up for my soul. He watches over me. I am a city set on a hill, and my glory can be neither displaced nor hidden. Angels are on guard; my feet are kept from falling, and my soul is preserved to prosper. I remain in health, and I walk in divine health. My body remains in strength. I have wisdom, and I am a man of understanding. My mind is profitable, for I have the mind of Christ. I am created for glory.

In Jesuss name, I believe and say amen.

Selected Affirmations

I am hidden in the hollow of the hand of the Almighty. Nothing makes me afraid. I have found my peace in the shadow of His wings.

Suggested Scriptures

Yea, though I walk through the valley of the shadow of death, I will fear no evil: for thou art with me; thy rod and thy staff they comfort me. (Psalm 23:4)

The Lord is my strength and my shield; my heart trusted in him, and I am helped: therefore my heart greatly rejoiceth; and with my song will I praise him. (Psalm 28:7)
Nor for the pestilence that walketh in darkness; nor for the destruction that wasteth at noonday. A thousand shall fall at thy side, and ten thousand at thy right hand; but it shall not come nigh thee. (Psalm 91:67)

Since thou wast precious in my sight, thou hast been honourable, and I have loved thee: therefore will I give men for thee, and people for thy life. (Isaiah 43:4)

40. Divine Turnaround

Today, I speak over my life and my household that God changes our story so we experience a divine turnaround.

As my life takes on a new meaning, my tests have become testimonies, I am triumphant in all my trials, and my pain has turned into power. I am not a victimI have become a victor. God has changed my times and seasons, and I emerge suddenly to fulfill destiny. I access the fullness of Gods mercy by the power in the name and the blood of Jesus. I am redeemed by grace, and I am strengthened by my faith. I am preserved by the power in the righteous right hand of my God. I have no fear, for God loves me perfectly. I break through every barrier of limitation, and I break forth on every side. My confidence is in the grace of God. I can do all things through Christ, who strengthens me. I am covered with favor as with a shield; I am led of the spirit into all truth. I have the keys of David. Heaven and the earth answer to me. I have the oil of ease, so nothing is difficult or impossible for me. I am a believer. The sun of righteousness with healing in His wings arises on me today. I access the balm of Gilead, and pain and discomfort of every kind disappear. I receive the enabling power of the Holy Spirit to excel in wisdom, and I am perfected in the counsel of His will. I prosper in all that I do. I am directed to profit as I access the storehouses of divine wealth. The earth yields its increase to me. I am established in abundance. I am immune to failure; success is attracted to me. I have great success.

In Jesuss name, I believe and say amen.

Selected Affirmations

As my life takes on a new meaning, my tests have become testimonies, I am triumphant in all my trials, and my pain has turned into power. I am not a victim, for I have become a victor.

Suggested Scriptures

When the Lord turned again the captivity of Zion, we were like them that dream. (Psalm 126:1)

That the trial of your faith, being much more precious than of gold that perisheth, though it be tried with fire, might be found unto praise and honour and glory at the appearing of Jesus Christ. (1 Peter 1:7)

Fear thou not; for I am with thee: be not dismayed; for I am thy God: I will strengthen thee; yea, I will help thee; yea, I will uphold thee with the right hand of my righteousness. (Isaiah 41:10)

But unto you that fear my name shall the Sun of righteousness arise with healing in his wings; and ye shall go forth, and grow up as calves of the stall. (Malachi 4:2)

41. Answered Prayers

Today, I speak over my life and my household that God turns His ears to our cries and grants the desires of our hearts.

I delight myself in the Lord always. My eyes are on Him perpetually. I will not be disappointed, and the expectations of my heart will not be denied. I have the fulfillment of my dreams, for my goals are attainable and my prayers are answered. God is my helper, and I have space in His presence. I do not return empty; my needs are met according to His riches in glory in Christ Jesus. Angels watch over my every step, so I will not dash my foot against the stone. My walk is protected; I dip my feet in butter, and the rock pours out for me rivers of oil. My steps are ordered by God, and He leads me on the path of righteousness for His names sake. I am not stranded or forsaken, God is my keeper and my strength. I am sanctified by the blood of the everlasting covenant. My hands lay hold of the horns of the altar, and the avenger of blood cannot reach me. The power in the name of Jesus distinguishes me; I am set apart for elevation, I am marked for greatness, and good things happen to me always. I overcome every challenge; I will not fall. I am the recipient of Gods grace. I am blessed in all my ways. My sins are forgiven. I am the righteousness of God in Christ Jesus.

In Jesuss name, I believe and say amen.

SELECTED AFFIRMATIONS

I will not be disappointed; the expectations of my heart will not be denied.

SUGGESTED SCRIPTURES

Delight thyself also in the Lord: and he shall give thee the desires of thine heart. (Psalm 37:4)

For surely there is an end; and thine expectation shall not be cut off. (Proverbs 23:18)

But my God shall supply all your need according to his riches in glory by Christ Jesus. (Philippians 4:19)

They shall bear thee up in their hands, lest thou dash thy foot against a stone. (Psalm 91:12)

42. I Have a Willing Spirit

Today, I speak over my life and my household that God adds to us and that the Almighty grants us access to the fullness of His bounty.

Gods will is perfected in my life, and His mercy extends to me. I stand in line for the manifestation of His power; nothing separates me from the love of the Lord. I am established in the light of His covenant, washed in the blood of the cross, and sealed by the power of His precious spirit. I come as it is written of me in the volume of the books to do His will. I experience His power afresh. I do His good pleasure, for I have the willing spirit. I am endued and endowed by His grace. There is nothing difficult for me; He is my God, and nothing is impossible with Him. I enter into the realm of possibilities, and I move into a season of divine assistance. I am helped; I have angelic support and the backing of the heavenly hosts. I have the oil of ease and the supply of the spirit. As I go forward, nothing hinders me, for I have divine acceleration. The plowman overtakes the reaper, the one who treads grapes overtakes the sower, the hills melt, and the mountain drops sweet wine for me. It is a new day, a brand-new season, and the disappointments of the past are swallowed up by the faithfulness of the Lord. Victory is perpetuated in my life, and I march on from victory unto victory in Christ Jesus. I build and inhabit, I eat of my own gardens, and my children surround my table. I am immune to failure.

In Jesuss name, I believe and say amen.

Selected Affirmations

It is a new day, a brand-new season, and the disappointments of the past are swallowed up by the faithfulness of the Lord. Victory is perpetuated in my life.

Suggested Scriptures

And David said unto Gad, I am in a great strait: let us fall now into the hand of the Lord; for his mercies are great: and let me not fall into the hand of man. (2 Samuel 24:14)

And from Jesus Christ, who is the faithful witness, and the first begotten of the dead, and the prince of the kings of the earth. Unto him that loved us, and washed us from our sins in his own blood. (Revelation 1:5)

And Jesus looking upon them saith, With men it is impossible, but not with God: for with God all things are possible. (Mark 10:27)

Behold, the days come, saith the Lord, that the plowman shall overtake the reaper, and the treader of grapes him that soweth seed; and the mountains shall drop sweet wine, and all the hills shall melt. (Amos 9:13)

43. I Have Refuge in His Name

Today, I speak over my life and my household that God covers us with as with a shield and keeps us from evil as He has promised.

I find refuge in the name of the Lord; I run into it and am safe. I hide in the cleft of the rock, and no harm befalls me. Nothing hurts me, for the Lord is my light and my salvation. I fear no one, for the Lord is the strength of my life. I am not afraid, for I am kept in the secret place of the most high. I dwell under the shadow of the Almighty, and the Lord is my cover, my fortress, my trust, and my hope. He is my hiding place. The cords and chains of death are broken; the Lord has freed me. He is my song and my victory, He is my succor in the times of weariness, and He is my banner in the days of battle. I am stronger than my foes and wiser than the enemy. The Lord is always with me. He has not left me and will not leave me. My feet are on the necks of those that rise against me; by the power of the Lord I beat them face down and triumph over them. I have the victory over sin and death. Grace delivers me, God favors me, the earth yields abundance, mercy meets me, and Gods compassion accompanies me. God is my joy and peace, my song and dance, my sword and battle-ax. I excel in all my hands find to do. I am guarded by the hosts of heaven. I have the spirit of God, the spirit of wisdom and counsel, the spirit of the fear of God, and the spirit of knowledge and understanding. I cannot be prevented from destiny. I march on swiftly to the attainment of my purpose.

In Jesuss name, I believe and say amen.

Selected Affirmations

I dwell under the shadow of the Almighty; the Lord is my cover, my fortress, my trust, and my hope.

I hide in the cleft of the rock, and no harm befalls me.

Suggested Scriptures

The name of the Lord is a strong tower: the righteous runneth into it, and is safe. (Proverbs 18:10)

The Lord is my light and my salvation; whom shall I fear? the Lord is the strength of my life; of whom shall I be afraid? (Psalm 27:1)

He that dwelleth in the secret place of the most High shall abide under the shadow of the Almighty. (Psalm 91:1)

Thou hast also given me the necks of mine enemies; that I might destroy them that hate me. (Psalm 18:40)

44. Divine Inspiration

Today, I speak over my life and my household that God rules in our affairs and governs our lives; nothing can go wrong.

God is on my side, so I am a winner. The resurrection anointing is at work in my life, my dreams come alive, and my vision finds expression. I am divinely inspired by the breath of the Almighty. God will neither leave nor forsake me. He leads me into destiny, and I see my way through to the place of fulfillment. He guides me with the light of His countenance, and my path is illuminated by the light of His presence. The yoke of confusion dissipates with the brightness of the glory of my God. Mountains become as plains before me when I dwell in the presence of the Lord, and the hills melt like wax before me. I have the fullness of joy; the pleasure of His right hand breaks the yoke of pressure around me. I have the restoration of all things, things are turned around for my good, and the holding pattern over my life is broken. God shows me the way; I am led by the spirit. I am a son of God; I am royalty. I am backed and supported by the heavenly hosts. I have successfully come through the wilderness, and I walk into my promised land. The drought is over; I am entrenched in supernatural abundance and the blessing of God meets me at the right place. I am seated in the heavenly places in Christ Jesus. The dew of heaven brings to me the season of refreshing, and I see the revelation of His glory once more. I have a living hope. Gods plans for my future are of peace and not evil. I attain unto the purpose of God for my life. I am established as Gods regent.

In Jesuss name, I believe and say amen.

Selected Affirmations

He leads me into destiny, and I see my way through to the place of fulfillment; He guides me with the light of His countenance, and my path is illuminated by the light of His presence.

Suggested Scriptures

This matter is by the decree of the watchers, and the demand by the word of the holy ones: to the intent that the living may know that the most High ruleth in the kingdom of men, and giveth it to whomsoever he will, and setteth up over it the basest of men. (Daniel 4:17)

But if the Spirit of him that raised up Jesus from the dead dwell in you, he that raised up Christ from the dead shall also quicken your mortal bodies by his Spirit that dwelleth in you. (Romans 8:11)

And I will restore to you the years that the locust hath eaten, the cankerworm, and the caterpillar, and the palmerworm, my great army which I sent among you. (Joel 2:25)

But there is a spirit in man: and the inspiration of the Almighty giveth them understanding. (Job 32:8)

45. Established and Perfected

Today, I speak over my life and my household that God perfects and establishes us and that the Almighty strengthens and settles us as He has promised.

His mercy, grace, and love set me apart for a lift. I am a blessed man; the spirit of the living God dwells in me. I am set apart for good works, selected for His glory, and elevated for the establishment of divine purpose. I am a creation of maximum impact, created to add value for the benefit of this generation and generations yet unborn. I reign in life, for I was born to rule. All things are possible for me. My hands are strong for the fight. My feet run swiftly to success, my heart ponders the goodness of the Lord in the land of the living, and my mind is stayed on Him. I am kept in perfect peace. I am seated high above the principalities and powers of this age. Heaven favors my cause. The earth supports my efforts, men honor me, and God favors me. I am the righteousness of God in Christ Jesus. God is not my enemy; He is my Father. All things work in my favor; the curse is broken, and every disadvantage is reversed. I have the resurrection power of the Lord working for me. I have the answers to all my prayers; God is good to me always, and nothing is against me. Its harvest time, the season of restoration of all things; its a new season, the dawn of a new day. I see the manifestation of the counsel of His will. I am forever lifted, never to fall.

In Jesuss name, I believe and say amen.

Selected Affirmations

I am a creation of maximum impact, created to add value for the benefit of this generation and generations yet unborn.

Suggested Scriptures

But the God of all grace, who hath called us unto his eternal glory by Christ Jesus, after that ye have suffered a while, make you perfect, stablish, strengthen, settle you. (1 Peter 5:10)

Blessed be the God and Father of our Lord Jesus Christ, who hath blessed us with all spiritual blessings in heavenly places in Christ. (Ephesians 1:3)

For we are his workmanship, created in Christ Jesus unto good works, which God hath before ordained that we should walk in them. (Ephesians 2:10)

Far above all principality, and power, and might, and dominion, and every name that is named, not only in this world, but also in that which is to come. (Ephesians 1:21)

46. Fulfilled in Faith

Today, I speak over my life and my household that God helps us and that the Almighty vindicates us.

The Lord is my light and my song; He has become our salvation. I am not afraid, for I remain confident in the faithfulness of God. I am not forsaken, for God hears me when I call and answers when I cry. His loving kindness is extended to me. In all things I remain the cherished darling of the Lord, and I am guarded jealously as the apple of His eye. I am covered by the blood of the everlasting covenant, so I am delivered from sudden destruction and protected by an innumerable company of angels. God has taken away diseases far from me, His body was broken for me, and His blood was shed for the forgiveness of my sins, so I have a clean slate, a new start. I am not in enmity with God; I am reconciled with the creator of all flesh. Life takes a new meaning: all things work together for my good, everything is turning around for my good, and nothing is against me. My future is secure in Him, and my destiny is delivered; I am divinely empowered for purpose. Grace is granted, mercy manifests to me, and I find fulfillment in faith. The joy of the Lord is my strength, and the power of His love has saved me from death. I live because He lives also. I am created a sign and an amazing wonder unto many; the sons of the stranger are my vine dressers, and many will serve me. Every insurrection of the enemy against my destiny is destroyed, and every conspiracy against my purpose is discomfited. I mount with wings like the eagle, I wax valiant in battle, and I am victorious in life. I am favored by God, and I am honored by men. God lifts me. I move into position. The spirit that raised Christ from the dead is at work in me.

In Jesuss name, I believe and say amen.

Selected Affirmations

Life takes a new meaning: all things work together for my good, everything is turning around for my good, and nothing is against me.

Suggested Scriptures

He shall see of the travail of his soul, and shall be satisfied: by his knowledge shall my righteous servant justify many; for he shall bear their iniquities. (Isaiah 53:11)

And it shall come to pass, that before they call, I will answer; and while they are yet speaking, I will hear. (Isaiah 65:24)

And we know that all things work together for good to them that love God, to them who are the called according to his purpose. (Romans 8:28)

So David waxed greater and greater: for the Lord of hosts was with him. (1 Chronicles 11:9)

47. Claiming Territories

Today, I speak over my life and my household that God releases us into the fullness of His promises.

The mighty hand of God is upon me, and the word of the Lord finds me, so the chains of limitation are shattered off my hands, the shackles of stagnation taken off my feet and destroyed. I lift my hands and receive the best that God has prepared for me. I touch all that is reserved for me, and I achieve all that is written of me in the volume of the book. I walk freely into the place of honor. Everywhere the soles of my feet walk is taken as an inheritance. I cannot be locked out anymore; I cannot be shut out anymore. The Son of God has set me free, and I am free indeed. When I enter into my prepared place, I access the power in the presence of God and find help in the time of need. I have the fullness of joy and the eternal pleasures of His right hand. My strength is renewed; I rise yet again, my sun will not set at noon, and I break forth on every side. I am a city set on a hill; my mountain drips of milk, wine, and honey; my feet are dipped in butter; and the rock pours for me rivers of oil. God lifts my head higher than those of my foes. I am not abandoned, for God is with me. I am not forsaken, for God has favored me. I am not forgotten, for God has remembered me. I am accepted in the beloved, I am celebrated and not simply tolerated, and my best days are still ahead of me. God is the covering of my head in the days of battle. I have the victory; I am a winner. I am a gift of God to my generation, and purpose is fulfilled in my life. The top of my mountains are now visible, and the glory of God shines forth in my life.

In Jesuss name, I believe and say amen.

SELECTED AFFIRMATIONS

Everywhere the soles of my feet walk is taken as an inheritance.

The mighty hand of God is upon me, the word of the Lord finds me, the chains of limitation are shattered off my hands, and the shackles of stagnation are taken off my feet and destroyed.

SUGGESTED SCRIPTURES

Blessed be the Lord, that hath given rest unto his people Israel, according to all that he promised: there hath not failed one word of all his good promise, which he promised by the hand of Moses his servant. (1 Kings 8:56)

And when he came unto Lehi, the Philistines shouted against him: and the Spirit of the Lord came mightily upon him, and the cords that were upon his arms became as flax that was burnt with fire, and his bands loosed from off his hands. (Judges 15:14)

By humility and the fear of the Lord are riches, and honour, and life. (Proverbs 22:4)

Every place whereon the soles of your feet shall tread shall be yours: from the wilderness and Lebanon, from the river, the river Euphrates, even unto the uttermost sea shall your coast be. (Deuteronomy 11:24)

48. God of My Process

Today, I speak over my life and my household that the power of the Holy Spirit comes upon us that and the hand of God stays on our lives for good.

I receive the anointing of the Holy Ghost that makes the impossible a possibility. I am set apart for the supernatural and not for the mundane. Gods plan for my life is still intact; I will not be stranded, for He is the God of my process. He has neither left nor forsaken me. I rejoice in the presence of my God, Christ, King, and Heavenly Father always. Like the Lord I return in the power of the spirit, my renown spreads far and abroad, and my influence and impact are global. I am a child of promise, a son of consolation. I bring solutions, and my generation and succeeding generations will yet hear from me. I will fulfill my purpose. Heaven influences my decision; I am led by the Holy Spirit. I am a child of God, I am blessed by God, and I am the righteousness of God in Christ Jesus. I am called with a higher calling, marked for an eternity with Christ, commended unto good works, born a royalty, and created a success. I emerge a prince of power with God. Nothing holds me down; no one keeps me under. I rise unto the perfection of Gods glory for my life, a life of peace, plenty, and unceasing progress. Every day is an improvement on the increase of the revelation of Gods goodness in my life; my path shines brighter and brighter unto the perfect day. The dawn of a new season is here, and I see everything turn around for my own good. I am a city set on a hill, the light of the world, and the salt of the earth. I am a change agent, a minister of the grace of God. The spirit that raised Christ from the dead is at work in me.

In Jesuss name, I believe and say amen.

Selected Affirmations

Every day is an improvement on the increase of the revelation of Gods goodness in my life; my path shines brighter and brighter unto the perfect day.

Heaven influences my decision; I am led by the Holy Spirit.

Suggested Scriptures

And the angel answered and said unto her, The Holy Ghost shall come upon thee, and the power of the Highest shall overshadow thee: therefore also that holy thing which shall be born of thee shall be called the Son of God. (Luke 1:35)

For the Lord will not forsake his people for his great names sake: because it hath pleased the Lord to make you his people. (1 Samuel 12:22)

Now also when I am old and grey headed, O God, forsake me not; until I have shewed thy strength unto this generation, and thy power to every one that is to come. (Psalm 71:18)

So shall thy barns be filled with plenty, and thy presses shall burst out with new wine. (Proverbs 3:10)

49. Breaking the Chains of Delay

Today, I speak over my life and my household that Gods prophetic visitation lifts us to where we belong.

His mercy exalts my head in this season. The chains of delay are broken, and I am free to fly; I am emancipated. I reach for the establishment of Gods promises in my life, and I am anointed with fresh oil. The grace of prophesy jet-propels me into the manifestation of Gods glory. From this point onward, as I go forward I am favored by God and men, and men honor me wherever I turn. Every dry area receives the release of the dew of heaven; I have abundant rain, the latter and the former together, and I see increase all around me. I walk into the grace of completion, and I am not denied, for God sustains me and my mouth is filled with good things. God is at work in me to will and do His good pleasure. I eat the good of this land. I am numbered among the mighty, I share and partake of the lot of the strong, my borders are extended, the gates of brass are broken, and the bars of iron are cut asunder. I have access into the secret riches of hidden places, I have the outpouring of the seven-fold spirit of God; I have the spirit of wisdom, knowledge, counsel, might, the fear of God, the spirit of understanding, and the spirit of the Lord. I am a man of quick understanding in the fear of the Lord. I drink of the river that makes glad the city of God. I am planted in the garden of God. My leaves do not wither; I bring forth my fruit abundantly in and out of season. I am a profitable servant. I am a blessing to mankind. I am purpose driven. God is in charge of my process. I will make it. The spirit that raised Christ from the dead is at work in me. The top of my mountains are now visible, and the glory of God shines forth in my life.

In Jesuss name, I believe and say amen.

SELECTED AFFIRMATIONS

Every dry area receives the release of the dew of heaven. I have abundant rain, the latter and the former together; I see increase all around me. I walk into the grace of completion.

SUGGESTED SCRIPTURES

For thou art the glory of their strength: and in thy favour our horn shall be exalted. (Psalm 89:17)

But my horn shalt thou exalt like the horn of an unicorn: I shall be anointed with fresh oil. (Psalm 92:10)

Who satisfieth thy mouth with good things; so that thy youth is renewed like the eagles. (Psalm 103:5)

And I will give thee the treasures of darkness, and hidden riches of secret places, that thou mayest know that I, the Lord, which call thee by thy name, am the God of Israel. (Isaiah 45:3)

50. Prosperity from Coast to Coast

Today, I speak over my life and my household that the power of the Lord delivers us and that His glory covers us.

I am created in the righteousness of the Lord. I have been rescued from shame, destruction, and damnation, for I am saved by the blood of the everlasting covenant. God is my protection and the covering of my head in the day of battle, so when I lift up the banner of the Lord, I am victorious. I experience divine turnaround, and my head is raised higher than those of my foes. My eyes are fixed firmly on my goal, my feet are anointed for good, and I walk into divinely prepared provision where lack is swallowed up in abundance. I receive grace for Gods establishment in all I do; I prosper from coast to coast. My feet are secure on the land; I remain unmovable, my posterity intact. I am perfectly guarded by the angelic host, and no evil shall befall me, for my mountain stand strong. My life is a plus to creation; I add value to Gods plan in my generation. I am a sign and a wonder to many; I have access to the keys of the kingdom, and I possess the gates of my enemies. I am accepted in the beloved; I am favored; and wisdom, understanding, and knowledge are given to me without measure. I see the desires of my heart on my enemies. Every conspiracy against my destiny is destroyed for my sake, every psychic command against me is overturned, every soulful prayer against my person is overruled, and the heavens reject the counsel of the wicked over my family. Gods glory is made manifest over us. I shall live and not die. I am the head and not the tail, I am established as a force of righteousness, and God fights my battles. I am blessed by the Lord. It is a new season for me.

In Jesuss name, I believe and say amen.

Selected Affirmations

I walk into divinely prepared provision, lack is swallowed up in abundance. I receive grace for Gods establishment in all I do.

I am favored; wisdom, understanding, knowledge are given to me without measure.

Suggested Scriptures

They shall not be ashamed in the evil time: and in the days of famine they shall be satisfied. (Psalm 37:19)

But thanks be to God, which giveth us the victory through our Lord Jesus Christ. (1 Corinthians 15:57)

Lord, by thy favour thou hast made my mountain to stand strong: thou didst hide thy face, and I was troubled. (Psalm 30:7)

That in blessing I will bless thee, and in multiplying I will multiply thy seed as the stars of the heaven, and as the sand which is upon the sea shore; and thy seed shall possess the gate of his enemies. (Genesis 22:17)

51. Divine Direction

Today, I speak over my life and my household that God is for us and that no man is against us.

Nothing can separate me from the love of God in Christ Jesus, and I am alive to the promises of God. I increase daily in the love, wisdom, grace, and revelation knowledge of the most-high God. The Lord is my defense and my shield; He is the hedge of protection around me. My eyes are fixed on Him, and when I look to the Lord I will not see shame. I am submerged in the sea of His mercy, and His loving kindness to me is better than life itself. The Lord fixes the brightness of His countenance over me; my path is flooded with light, and I do not walk in darkness. Everything is working out for my good, and I get more than I expect from the Lord. He exceeds my expectation every time; I am comforted on all sides. I look up, lifting my eyes beyond the hills, and see that my help is from God. My helpers are God-ordained, divine help is my portion, and my helpers locate me. I am divinely directed, so I am at the right place at the right time. I progress, and I am elevated. My election is sure, my triumph certain, my victory constant. My vision is eternal, and nothing hampers or hinders the flow of Gods spirit in my direction. I am ordained for success, created for every good work of God in Christ Jesus, destined by heaven and relevant to earthly life. I am a minister of life and the divine graces of God; I am a child of consolation and one born in season. Its my time, and its my turn. I have divine acceleration; like an arrow shot out of a bow of steel, I will not miss the mark. I rise above the realm of impossibility and difficulty. I have the oil of ease and the grace of divine possibility; nothing is against me. All things work together for my good. God will not forsake me.

In Jesuss name, I believe and say amen.

Selected Affirmations

I am divinely directed; I am at the right place at the right time. I progress, I am elevated, my election is sure, my triumph is certain, and my victory is constant.

Suggested Scriptures

What shall we then say to these things? If God be for us, who can be against us? (Romans 8:31)

Because thy lovingkindness is better than life, my lips shall praise thee. (Psalm 63:3)

Now unto him that is able to do exceeding abundantly above all that we ask or think, according to the power that worketh in us. (Ephesians 3:20)

And the hand of the Lord was on Elijah; and he girded up his loins, and ran before Ahab to the entrance of Jezreel. (1 Kings 18:46)

52. I Am Spirit Led

Today, I speak over my life and my household that God shines the light of His presence over us.

His wisdom leads me into all truth, and I do not stumble on the path in my walk. I see my way through; I have clarity of thought. God has not given me the spirit of slavery again to fear; I have the spirit of love and power, and I have a sound mind. I have the mind of Christ so I can be like Him. He who knew no sin became sin, so I am the righteousness of God in Christ Jesus. I have access to the presence by the blood of the everlasting covenant, and I have grace to help in the time of need. I am not on my own, for God is with me; I am led by the spirit. I am lifted and seated in heavenly places, far above the powers of this world and age. God covers me, so I am completely protected. I am divinely enabled and eternally empowered by the spirit of God. My hands prosper in all I do; I live my dreams, my vision is enabled, and I am established in purpose. My God-ordained destiny is intact; I am set on the track of divine fulfillment. I am not forsaken, and my seed will not beg for bread. My wait is not in vain, for the day of my appointment is here. God hears me when I call, and I have the answers to my prayers. My requests are granted, and I have the desires of my heart. I see the way out, frustration has come to an end, and the expectation of my heart shall not be cut off; I am marvelously helped. I am significant in my generation, for God marks me for constant lifting, and shouts of victory and rejoicing resound in my household. The Lords right hand does mighty things for me. I am selected for breakthroughs, the two-leaved gates are opened, and the bars of iron are shattered.

In Jesuss name, I believe and say amen.

Selected Affirmations

I have the spirit of love and power, and I have a sound mind. I have the mind of Christ so I can be like Him.

Suggested Scriptures

When thou goest, thy steps shall not be straitened; and when thou runnest, thou shalt not stumble. (Proverbs 4:12)

For he hath made him to be sin for us, who knew no sin; that we might be made the righteousness of God in him. (2 Corinthians 5:21)

For God hath not given us the spirit of fear; but of power, and of love, and of a sound mind. (2 Timothy 1:7)

I have been young, and now am old; yet have I not seen the righteous forsaken, nor his seed begging bread. (Psalm 37:25)

53. God, My Defense

Today, I speak over my life and my household that God perfects all that concern us and remains a rock and fortress for us.

God is my glory and the lifter of my head. God is the shield around me. There is no breach in the hedge of protection around me. God is my refuge and my strong tower. I abide under the shadow of the Almighty, I dwell in the secret place of the most high, and I trust in the Lord. I am not confused, and I will not be dismayed. No evil comes near my abode, for God is my defense and my buckler. Fear is defeated, and the power of His mercy and love reign over my life. His sweet spirit is in control, and everything aligns with the power of His will. Because He rules over the affairs of my life, I have supernatural peace nothing missing, nothing broken. I rest in hope, and abound in power; nothing is difficult or impossible for me, and nothing is against me. Time is on my side, for He makes all things beautiful in time for me. I have all that God has promised; I break forth on all sides, I have my destiny intact. My inheritance remains mine, I have not lost ground, and God is my exceedingly great reward. I have beauty in place of ashes and the garment of praise for the spirit of heaviness. Gods glory makes a way for me; I am not stranded. I have found favor; I am distinguished and held in honor. The Lord my God is my sun and shield, He gives me grace and shows me His glory, and good is not withheld from me. This is my appointed time; this is my due season. My coast is enlarged, and my borders are extended. God grants my requests; my prayers are answered. I am accepted in the beloved. I have more than I bargained for. I am in health. I will make it. The spirit that raised Christ from the dead is at work in me.

In Jesuss name, I believe and say amen.

Selected Affirmations

God is my refuge and my strong tower. I abide under the shadow of the Almighty.

The Lord my God is my sun and shield.

Suggested Scriptures

God is my strength and power: and he maketh my way perfect. (2 Samuel 22:33)

But thou, O Lord, art a shield for me; my glory, and the lifter up of mine head. (Psalm 3:3)

He only is my rock and my salvation; he is my defence; I shall not be greatly moved. (Psalm 62:2)

For thou shalt break forth on the right hand and on the left; and thy seed shall inherit the Gentiles, and make the desolate cities to be inhabited. (Isaiah 54:3)

54. Blessings Restored

Today, I speak over my life and my household that God preserves us for His names sake.

I am covered by the Lord for posterity, and every disadvantage is turned around for me; I have divine exemption from every generational setback. I am the redeemed of the Lord; I am bought back with the blood of the lamb, regenerated by the holy spirit of God. I have the life of God in me. I am restored to the heights of the blessings of God at Creation. I am a creation of the grace of the living God, loaded with the manifold goodness of the Lord. I am kept by the love of the most high. I am made for the manifestation of His power, forgiven by the counsel of His will, granted mercy by the power of His loving kindness, and raised in glory by the spirit of resurrection. I have received the gifts of the Father, and I am selected to do good works by the power of God. I have an excellent spirit. I grow in righteousness; increase in faith; and have the spirit of wisdom, power, and discretion. I am a child of God, and the spirit of adoption accords me the rights and privileges of sonship. I am free from the influences and workings of the law of sin and death. I live by grace and the spirit of life in Christ Jesus. The blessings of Abraham are restored to me, and the blessings of the heavenly places are mine. I have access to all things that are of God, for God is in charge of my process. I will make it.

In Jesuss name, I believe and say amen.

Selected Affirmations

I am restored to the heights of the blessings of God at Creation.

Suggested Scriptures

Nevertheless he saved them for his names sake, that he might make his mighty power to be known. (Psalm 106:8)

Let the redeemed of the Lord say so, whom he hath redeemed from the hand of the enemy. (Psalm 107:2)

They shall be carried to Babylon, and there shall they be until the day that I visit them, saith the Lord; then will I bring them up, and restore them to this place. (Jeremiah 27:22)

Then this Daniel was preferred above the presidents and princes, because an excellent spirit was in him; and the king thought to set him over the whole realm. (Daniel 6:3)

55. Lifted beyond Measure

Today, I speak over my life and my household that God elevates us past every point of our expectation and lifts us beyond measure.

The power of Gods mercy has liberated me from every form of oppression and defeated every form of opposition round about; more numerous are those who are with me than those who are against me. I am supported by the angels of heaven in every area of my life. God is my shield and my defense; no weapon formed against me shall prosper, and every tongue that rises against me is condemned already. Gods steadfast love toward me is ceaseless, the flow of His tender mercies in my life endless; I bask in the sea of His glorious wisdom. I emerge victorious in every battle because He fights all my battles; I have peace that passes all understanding. When I look to Him I do not see shame. I am delivered because I am the darling of the Lord. He is faithful. He is my King, God, and Heavenly Father. God is my source, so lack is swallowed up in abundance. The storehouses of heaven are opened to me, so I feast continually from the choicest of His divine provision. I am perfectly provided for, so I shall not want. I am led by His spirit, so I am not lost. God is my light, so confusion is destroyed. I am directed by His wisdom, so I know no loss. Grace and peace are multiplied to me, I am selected for a glorious future, I am marked for progress, and I have an excellent spirit; I am marvelously helped. God is the strength of my life and my portion, my promise keeper, and the redeemer of my soul. I am blessed because I am a blessing to the world. Nothing is impossible for me, because I am a believer. I will make it.

In Jesuss name, I believe and say amen.

Selected Affirmations

God is my source, so lack is swallowed up in abundance. The storehouses of heaven are opened to me, so I feast continually from the choicest of His divine provision. I am perfectly provided for, so I shall not want.

Suggested Scriptures

For the oppression of the poor, for the sighing of the needy, now will I arise, saith the Lord; I will set him in safety from him that puffeth at him. (Psalm 12:5)

No weapon that is formed against thee shall prosper; and every tongue that shall rise against thee in judgment thou shalt condemn. This is the heritage of the servants of the Lord, and their righteousness is of me, saith the Lord. (Isaiah 54:17)

Remember, O Lord, thy tender mercies and thy lovingkindnesses; for they have been ever of old. (Psalm 25:6)

And the peace of God, which passeth all understanding, shall keep your hearts and minds through Christ Jesus. (Philippians 4:7)

56. My Secure Inheritance

Today, I speak over my life and my household that God enlarges our borders and extends our boundaries.

I possess every ground my feet walk on as an inheritance from the Lord according to His promise. My heritage is in place; nothing subverts me from my cause, for I am assisted by God. To the end that my vision is empowered, I have divine provision; God is my source, and I have an unlimited flow of Gods grace in my life. I remain unstoppable. My shoulders are relieved of the heavy basket, the burden is lifted, and the yoke is broken and destroyed by the anointing of the Holy Spirit. I am at liberty; I am free to fly. I am jet-propelled into my destiny. I have divine acceleration, the grace to outrun the chariots and horses, and the grace to excel and prosper beyond every man-made limit set for my life. I see beyond the cloud; I enter into and am established in the zone of ceaseless possibilities and limitless potential. The oil of ease and gladness make all things possible, and I have great success, for Gods glory manifests in me. I shine like the stars in the night. I arise, for my light is come, and kings come to the brightness of my rising and the world feels the impact of the power of my emergence. I am a man of influence, for I radiate the light of Gods unfailing word. Gods hand is upon me for good; I was created to do His will, and I show forth the power of His love. I receive mercy, and I have the joy of the Lord. My joy is full, and I am strengthened. Doors open for me, favor follows me, and I have the peace of God and know that nothing is broken, nothing is missing.

In Jesuss name, I believe and say amen.

Selected Affirmations

I possess every ground my feet walk on as an inheritance from the Lord according to His promise.

I enter into and am established in the zone of ceaseless possibilities and limitless potential.

Suggested Scriptures

And Jabez called on the God of Israel, saying, Oh that thou wouldest bless me indeed, and enlarge my coast, and that thine hand might be with me, and that thou wouldest keep me from evil, that it may not grieve me! And God granted him that which he requested. (1 Chronicles 4:10)

In whom also we have obtained an inheritance, being predestinated according to the purpose of him who worketh all things after the counsel of his own will. (Ephesians 1:11)

And it shall come to pass in that day, that his burden shall be taken away from off thy shoulder, and his yoke from off thy neck, and the yoke shall be destroyed because of the anointing. (Isaiah 10:27)

Now the Lord is that Spirit: and where the Spirit of the Lord is, there is liberty. (2 Corinthians 3:17)

57. Shielded by His Blood

Today, I speak over my life and my household that God is our God and our guide from now even unto the end.

I am surrounded by a multitude of angels, and the enemy cannot access any area of my life. The power in the name and the blood of the everlasting covenant totally shield me from any attack of the enemy. The Lord is my shepherd, and I shall not lack any good thing, for I am established in abundance. I am led by His spirit into safety, and all I have lost is restored to me. God is my righteousness by grace, and I shall not fear in the darkness of the valley or in the confusion of uncertainty. In the time of trouble, God defends me and lifts me. I have been redeemed of the Lord; I have been set free to serve Him without fear. My iniquity has been pardoned, my sins are forgiven, and a glorious future is assured; the rest of my days are as a shining light. I achieve purpose, for God has favored me all over again. I am set apart for glory, distinguished for the manifestation of His glory, and marked for global prominence. I am a person of impact in my generation; I am a city set on a hill; my light cannot be hidden, for I shine like the stars of heaven. Its harvest time, and I receive the bounty of Gods storehouses and call in the double portion blessing. Everything works in my favor; I move into my season of unfettered increase, unending progress, and unlimited breakthroughs. Doors of opportunities open up, my name is mentioned in the places that matter, and my joy is full. God shows me mercy, I do not lack divine inspiration, and I have the mind of Christ. My life is hidden in Christ and in God. No evil eye sees me or hands touch me, for I am jealously guarded as the apple of Gods eye.

In Jesuss name, I believe and say amen.

Selected Affirmations

The power in the name and the blood of the everlasting covenant totally shields me from any attack of the enemy.

Suggested Scriptures

But ye are come unto mount Sion, and unto the city of the living God, the heavenly Jerusalem, and to an innumerable company of angels. (Hebrews 12:22)

That at the name of Jesus every knee should bow, of things in heaven, and things in earth, and things under the earth. (Philippians 2:10)

Yea, though I walk through the valley of the shadow of death, I will fear no evil: for thou art with me; thy rod and thy staff they comfort me. (Psalm 23:4)

And they that be wise shall shine as the brightness of the firmament; and they that turn many to righteousness as the stars for ever and ever. (Daniel 12:3)

58. My Song of Thanksgiving

Today, I speak over my life and my household that God fills our mouths with praise and our hearts with thanksgiving.

When men said a casting down, the Lord has lifted me up. God makes a difference in my life and has distinguished me from my peers. His ears are open to my cry, and my prayers have been answered; I testify to Gods goodness to me in the land of the living. I am delivered from eternal damnation, I am redeemed from death and destruction, and I am a candidate of Gods mercy. I have peace with the Father of all spirits, and I have been reconciled with the God of all flesh; God is not my enemy. My sinful nature and sins are forgiven, and God smiles at me. I am bought back with a price: the blood of the everlasting covenant speaks for me, and there is therefore now no condemnation for me. God is my Father, the Lord is my strength and my song of thanksgiving, and He has become my salvation. My gaze is fixed on Him. He has delivered me from shame, and my tongue praises His name. His faithfulness to me is eternal, and my horn is exalted like the horn of a unicorn. My walls are protected; I have a living hope and a glorious future. I have a sound mind, the mind of Christ, for I am washed in the blood and cleansed by the washing of the water by the word. I am saved by grace through faith. God loves me endlessly, I have a brand-new life, and today is my day of visitation. I am blessed beyond the curse. I rejoice in the love of God and His everlasting mercy.

In Jesuss name, I believe and say amen.

Selected Affirmations

The blood of the everlasting covenant speaks for me; there is therefore now no condemnation for me. God is my Father, and the Lord is my strength and my song of thanksgiving.

Suggested Scriptures

Let my mouth be filled with thy praise and with thy honour all the day. (Psalm 71:8)

When men are cast down, then thou shalt say, There is lifting up; and he shall save the humble person. (Job 22:29)

I had fainted, unless I had believed to see the goodness of the Lord in the land of the living. (Psalm 27:13)

There is therefore now no condemnation to them which are in Christ Jesus, who walk not after the flesh, but after the Spirit. (Romans 8:1)

59. The Power of His Promise

Today, I speak over my life and my household that Gods grace is released to us and that His tender mercies are our portion eternally.

I receive the fullness of His love, and I walk in the power of His spirit; I have dominion, I multiply, and I increase on all sides. Gods word work wonders in my life, and I experience comfort in every area of my life. I have the peace of God that passes understanding; wisdom and knowledge are given to me in abundance. I walk in the power of Gods covenant, so I have divine insurance; my life is protected, and I am secure in Him. My race ends in glory, I fulfill my purpose, and I am in right standing; God justifies me. My name is written with those that press on to the saving of their souls. I do not draw back into perdition; I walk in the spirit. I will not fail, for I have the courage to will and do of Gods pleasures. I am a man of faith, and God is pleased with me. My enemies are at peace with me; I pass through the waters and rivers, but they will not overflow me. Through the fire I shall not be burned, neither shall the flame come upon me because God is with me. The glory of the Lord is risen upon me. I am shielded on all sides, protected, and guided by the host of angels. My life is aligned with the will of God, so I cannot stray or be stranded. I am totally immersed in the sea of His love, I am submerged in the oil of His presence, and I am hid in the cleft of the rock. I have rest for my soul. I proceed and make progress in all that I do. My efforts are crowned with great successI am delivered and not defeated. All things are working in my favor.

In Jesuss name, I believe and say amen.

Selected Affirmations

I have the peace of God that passes understanding; wisdom and knowledge are given to me in abundance. I walk in the power of Gods covenant, so I have divine insurance; my life is protected.

Suggested Scriptures

Thou madest him to have dominion over the works of thy hands; thou hast put all things under his feet. (Psalm 8:6)

I have fought a good fight, I have finished my course, I have kept the faith. (2 Timothy 4:7)

But we are not of them who draw back unto perdition; but of them that believe to the saving of the soul. (Hebrews 10:39)

Arise, shine; for thy light is come, and the glory of the Lord is risen upon thee. (Isaiah 60:1)

60. I Am Restored

Today, I speak over my life and my household that God restores to us everything we have lost and restores us to our predestined place and position.

Life gives back to me, and the heavens are opened over my life. I see clearly visions of a glorious future and hear the voice of God expressly for divine direction. I do not grope for light as in darkness; the power of confusion over my life is broken. The power of the Holy Spirit leads me, and wherever I go I break through on all sides. I have access into the presence of the living God by the blood of the everlasting covenant, so I have found grace to help in the time of need. I am not forsaken; God will not abandon me. I walk in step with the God of my salvation; I am in agreement with His divine plan over my life. God is at work in me to will and to do His good pleasure; I have a willing spirit, and I walk in Gods power. The Father is with me, and I am confident in the promises of God. He is my source and my shield, my provider and my protector, my sun and my light, my glory and the lifter of my head. I am assisted and elevated. My faith is helped because His word is true. He is good to me, and I am accepted in the beloved. I have been numbered with the strong in the land, and my gifts make room for me. I trample over snakes and scorpions; I overcome all the power of the enemy. When I exercise my authority and walk in dominion, nothing hurts me, for I am clad in the whole armor of God. I stand in the day of battle; He fights my battles, and I hold my peace. I have the victory. God is merciful to me. God loves me first, so I cannot lose out in life. I am kept by God, so my life will not be lost.

In Jesuss name, I believe and say amen.

God restores to us everything we have lost and restores us to our predestined place and position.

SUGGESTED SCRIPTURES

And he restored the chief butler unto his butlership again; and he gave the cup into Pharaohs hand. (Genesis 40:21)

And it shall come to pass afterward, that I will pour out my spirit upon all flesh; and your sons and your daughters shall prophesy, your old men shall dream dreams, your young men shall see visions. (Joel 2:28)

Let us therefore come boldly unto the throne of grace, that we may obtain mercy, and find grace to help in time of need. (Hebrews 4:16)

A mans gift maketh room for him, and bringeth him before great men. (Proverbs 18:16)

61. The Safety of His Presence

Today, I speak over my life and my household that God remembers us for good and that the Almighty will not forsake us.

My future is in His hands; I am inscribed on the palm of His hands. God watches over me; He is the strength of my life and my portion forever, the wall of protection all around me, and my song in the night season so I am sustained till the break of dawn. A new day has come, this is a new season, and joy has come. The morning is here, and I am right in the center of Gods will. My life is framed by the word of faith, and I am an addition to creation. I am a person of impact; I add value to this generation and the generations yet unborn. I walk in divine revelation and see the power of God at work in my life. I am a sign and a wonder unto many as the recipient of Gods mercy and loving kindness; the grace of God distinguishes me. I am favored by God. I am blessed; the curse of the law is reversed, and I am authorized to progress and prosper in all I think of and do. My life is a testament of Gods goodness. I am the planting of God by the streams of living water; I am eternally fruitful. I dwell in the secret place of the most high, so I am safe from every trouble, hurt, and harm. I am everything God says I am; my destiny is real. God created and ordained me for purpose; I am not a disappointment to creation, for I operate under open heavens. Nothing is difficult for me, for I have the oil of His presence. Things happen for me easily: I shine like the sun, I surpass every human expectation set for me, and I have an excellent spirit. By the power of Gods spirit I exceed every boundary set by men. I fulfill the glorious destiny of God my creator.

In Jesus name, I believe and say amen.

Selected Affirmations

I dwell in the secret place of the most high, so I am safe from every trouble, hurt, and harm. I am everything God says I am; my destiny is real.

Suggested Scriptures

Behold, I have graven thee upon the palms of my hands; thy walls are continually before me. (Isaiah 49:16)

The Lord is my strength and my shield; my heart trusted in him, and I am helped: therefore my heart greatly rejoiceth; and with my song will I praise him. (Psalm 28:7)

For his anger endureth but a moment; in his favour is life: weeping may endure for a night, but joy cometh in the morning. (Psalm 30:5)

And he shall be like a tree planted by the rivers of water, that bringeth forth his fruit in his season; his leaf also shall not wither; and whatsoever he doeth shall prosper. (Psalm 1:3)

62. Distinguished by Faith

Today, I speak over my life and my household that God crowns our efforts with success and grants us a plentiful harvest of good things.

I am a fruitful bough; my branches grow over the wall. My feet are planted on the ground; I am established in the fullness of the covenant of Gods glorious promises. I have joy unspeakable, I am inspired by the breath of the Almighty, and the spirit of God finds expression in my life. The works of my hands are blessed, my feet are directed unto the path of greater effectiveness, and my lot is maintained in life. I am an heir of God and joint heir with Christ. I have an excellent spirit, I am distinguished by the spirit of faith, and I increase in the revelation of the Lord my God. I remain relevant to the scheme of God in this generation. The zeal of the Lord my God remains upon me, and I am entrenched in His love forever. I am led by the Lord and His perfect spirit. I walk in truth, and grace is poured out to me. I am a sheep of His pasture; my soul follows hard after Him, and I find rest and am comforted by His faithfulness. I am strengthened by the spirit of might in my inward man. My eyes are stayed on Him, so I will not see shame. The Lord is ever before me, and crooked places are made straight before me. The heavens drop down before me, and the skies pour down righteousness. I am raised in righteousness, for God directs all my ways. I do not seek the Lord in vain. I have more than I have bargained for. I am safe. God has blessed me beyond all expectations. The spirit that raised Christ from the dead is at work in me.

In Jesuss name, I believe and say amen.

SELECTED AFFIRMATIONS

The works of my hands are blessed, and my feet are directed unto the path of greater effectiveness.

I am distinguished by the spirit of faith; I increase in the revelation of the Lord my God.

SUGGESTED SCRIPTURES

Joseph is a fruitful bough, even a fruitful bough by a well; whose branches run over the wall. (Genesis 49:22)

Whom having not seen, ye love; in whom, though now ye see him not, yet believing, ye rejoice with joy unspeakable and full of glory. (1 Peter 1:8)

Seven days shalt thou keep a solemn feast unto the Lord thy God in the place which the Lord shall choose: because the Lord thy God shall bless thee in all thine increase, and in all the works of thine hands, therefore thou shalt surely rejoice. (Deuteronomy 16:15)

That he would grant you, according to the riches of his glory, to be strengthened with might by his Spirit in the inner man. (Ephesians 3:16)

63. God, My Sustenance

Today, I speak over my life and my household that God enhances vision in our hearts and strengthens us to fulfill the opportunities life presents to us.

I have a glorious future; I am created for purpose, and everything aligns for that fact. My life is established in the fullness of Gods great destiny set ahead of me. The counsel of God over my life stands sure, the Lord is committed to me, the power of His will sets me in place, and nothing can displace me. I am surrounded by the unfailing grace of heaven, totally unfettered to accelerate into the best God has in store for me. I stand complete in the fullness of the knowledge of Gods will for my life. God validates me, God is my victory, and I am kept alive to fulfill Gods agenda for my life. I activate the spirit of wisdom and revelation in God. I locate the end point in glory, and I place my life in Gods hand. I am on trackI run my race with the full expression of His truth. I am set free to be all God called me to be. I can do all things through Christ, who strengthens me. My dreams and visions are alive, and they find proper establishment. Gods hand is upon my life, so I am set over systems, nations, and kingdoms; I am powerfully helped. As I break out of the cocoon and enter into the best season of my life, I am sustained by the power of Gods spirit. I am supernaturally assisted. I am a sign and a wonder to many. My life is an increase to creation; I am a solution provider. God is my sustenance.

In Jesuss name, I believe and say amen.

Selected Affirmations

Gods hand is upon my life, so I am set over systems, nations, and kingdoms; I am powerfully helped.

I enter into the best season of my life, and I am sustained by the power of Gods spirit.

Suggested Scriptures

For I know the thoughts that I think toward you, saith the Lord, thoughts of peace, and not of evil, to give you an expected end. (Jeremiah 29:11)

Declaring the end from the beginning, and from ancient times the things that are not yet done, saying, My counsel shall stand, and I will do all my pleasure. (Isaiah 46:10)

That the God of our Lord Jesus Christ, the Father of glory, may give unto you the spirit of wisdom and revelation in the knowledge of him. (Ephesians 1:17)

I can do all things through Christ which strengtheneth me. (Philippians 4:13)

64. Lifted

Today, I speak over my life and my household that Gods thoughts over us are perfect and that His disposition toward us is favorable.

I am set up for a lift; God has commanded His blessing of life everlasting toward me, and my eyes behold the goodness of the Lord in the land of the living. Grace, mercy, goodness, and salvation from the God of the earth are my portion. I have the keys of David; Gods covenant with me is still in place, and I will not be displaced. I am protected; my walls are fortified by the might of the Holy One, and I shall never be moved. My vision is enhanced by the spirit of revelation, and my ways are prepared before the Lord. I was created for divine greatness; I move into my place, and my space is enlarged. I occupy, and I am established. I exceed every expectation, and I am favored by God in every area of my life. I am elevated by the might of the Lord, and the dew of heaven delivers a season of refreshing. I see the glory of the Lord. I am enveloped in righteousness, kept by the spirit of holiness, and protected and jealously guarded as the apple of Gods eye. I am a person of distinction, and I have an excellent spirit. The works of my hands prosper, and God promotes me. I am loved by God, my sins are forgiven, and God has pardoned my mistakes. I am raised in honor, and I see increase all around me. I abound unto every good work in Christ. I move into my own. The lines have fallen for me in pleasant places. I have a godly heritage, my inheritance is preserved by covenant, and my lot is maintained by Gods faithfulness.

In Jesuss name, I believe and say amen.

Selected Affirmations

I am elevated by the might of the Lord, and the dew of heaven delivers a season of refreshing.

Suggested Scriptures

For I know the thoughts that I think toward you, saith the Lord, thoughts of peace, and not of evil, to give you an expected end. (Jeremiah 29:11)

And the key of the house of David will I lay upon his shoulder; so he shall open, and none shall shut; and he shall shut, and none shall open. (Isaiah 22:22)

I have set the Lord always before me: because he is at my right hand, I shall not be moved. (Psalm 16:8)

I write unto you, little children, because your sins are forgiven you for his names sake. (1 John 2:12)

65. Stir Up the Gifts

Today, I speak over my life and my household that Gods purpose for my creation is attained and that every gift inherent in me is activated.

I awaken divine potential and make every dormant dream a reality by the working of Gods spirit. The heavens over me are opened, and I hear God expressly. I see visions of the Father, and I receive clarity of sight. The grace of completion and the power of the spirit enable me. When my eyes are fixed on the God of Zion, my helpers find me and I am marvelously assisted till my fame and renown spread abroad. I am not limited concerning Gods vision for my life. I receive the knowledge of witty inventions, I have the power to remain relevant and prominent globally, and I will not be derailed or sidetracked by lifes issues and circumstances. I walk in the grace of God till I live out the full implications of my God-ordained vision, I break the yoke of delay, and I wont be denied. My place in Gods scheme of things is sure; I live in the abundance of Gods revelation, and the word of God is not scarce to me. I am led by the spirit of God. I am a son of God, and I manifest the glory of the Father; I am a witness of the manifold blessing of the most high. I have access to the storehouses of heaven, for God is my source. The vision is provided for, and I am endowed with wisdom and might and enabled with power. I have light, and confusion is far from me. I am mightily helped. My life is preserved, and I will fulfill my destiny. God is my shield, my keeper, and the strength of my life. The zeal of the house of the Lord is upon me, and I am honored with favor. Nothing is difficult for me. I am perfect in His will.

In Jesuss name, I believe and say amen.

SELECTED AFFIRMATIONS

I awaken divine potential and make every dormant dream a reality by the working of Gods spirit.

I am not limited concerning Gods vision for my life. I receive the knowledge of witty inventions.

SUGGESTED SCRIPTURES

Wherefore I put thee in remembrance that thou stir up the gift of God, which is in thee by the putting on of my hands. (2 Timothy 1:6)

Now it came to pass in the thirtieth year, in the fourth month, in the fifth day of the month, as I was among the captives by the river of Chebar, that the heavens were opened, and I saw visions of God. (Ezekiel 1:1)

Being confident of this very thing, that he which hath begun a good work in you will perform it until the day of Jesus Christ. (Philippians 1:6)

For as many as are led by the Spirit of God, they are the sons of God. (Romans 8:14)

66. The Joy of Salvation

Today, I speak over my life and my household that God showers His love over us and shows us His mercy forever.

I have the joy of salvation, and the grace of God flows freely to me. God has reserved His favor for me, and I am preserved from destruction. I am the anointed of the Lord, set apart from the mundane for the glorious use of the Lord in the land of the living. I have a powerful vision, an amazing destiny, and the covenant of the Lord with me is still in place. My life is sustained by the force of His glory, and all things are in place for the establishment of my vision. I enter into a season of fulfillment of all that is written concerning me. God is my helper, I have the backing of heaven, and the angels stand by to carry out divine instructions on my behalf. I am created for the top. I am a city set on a hill, my feet are set upon the solid rock, and my mountain stands strong. I have great faith. My eyes are fixed upon the Lord; I am not distracted from my goal. God is the strength of my life and my portion forever. I mount with wings like the eagle, I run without fainting, and I walk without being weary. I get the best out of life, and I prosper in all my hands find to do. I am so blessed, I am a blessing. I am purchased by the blood of the everlasting covenant; I am cleansed by the water of the word. The Lord sees no sin in me and finds no iniquity about my life. I am forgiven, for I am the righteousness of God in Christ Jesus. I am justified, and my life is fortified by the power of the Lord. No evil comes near me, for the glory of the Lord is risen upon me. I am a source of joy to all I encounter, and I bring succor to many. I am a child of encouragement, I am a son of consolation, and I add value to creation.

In Jesuss name, I believe and say amen.

Selected Affirmations

I have a powerful vision, an amazing destiny, the covenant of the Lord with me is still in place.

My eyes are fixed upon the Lord, I am not distracted from my goal.

Suggested Scriptures

Restore unto me the joy of thy salvation; and uphold me with thy free spirit. (Psalm 51:12)

He sent his word, and healed them, and delivered them from their destructions. (Psalm 107:20)

Behold, God is mine helper: the Lord is with them that uphold my soul. (Psalm 54:4)

Now the God of peace, that brought again from the dead our Lord Jesus, that great shepherd of the sheep, through the blood of the everlasting covenant. (Hebrews 13:20)

67. God, My Maker

Today, I speak over my life and my household that God completes His work in us until the day of Christ and that He remembers His covenant for us.

I am neither forgotten nor forsaken; God perfects all that concerns me in His time. I am inscribed on the palm of His hands, and my life is in His hands. God is the strength of my life and my portion forever. He rules over my life; He is in control of my future and the author of my destiny. I am predestined for greatness; Gods righteous banner is raised over my life, and I manifest His glory. I do not miss out on Gods best for my life but arise to the glorious future preordained by God unto me. God smiles on me, and good things happen for me. I am the delight of the Father, and I see the goodness of the Lord in the land of the living. The limit is taken off me, the barrier is broken, and the chains are taken off my feet. I outrun the chariots and horses, I am supernaturally enabled, and I have divine acceleration. God is rich in grace toward me; I am favored above the rest. God fights my battles, and I enjoy the victory. I prosper in all that my hands find to do. I have the authority to trample on snakes and scorpions, I overcome all the power of the enemy, and nothing can hurt me. God is my defense and my fortress. I abide in safety continually. He sets my feet upon the solid rock. I have might and dominion. I pursue, overtake, and recover all, for this is my season of divine restoration. I have been vindicated by the God of heaven. I move into my own. I am not delayed anymore, for this is my time. The Lord has heard me, and He has set me as a sign and a wonder; I am a blessing to my generation. My boughs reach above the walls, my coat is of many colors, and my reach is to diverse nations and nationalities. My life is kept.

In Jesuss name, I believe and say amen.

Selected Affirmations

I am inscribed on the palm of His hands, and my life is in His hands. God is the strength of my life and my portion forever. He rules over my life; He is in control of my future and the author of my destiny.

Suggested Scriptures

And ye are complete in him, which is the head of all principality and power. (Colossians 2:10)

Behold, I have graven thee upon the palms of my hands; thy walls are continually before me. (Isaiah 49:16)

He brought me forth also into a large place; he delivered me, because he delighted in me. (Psalm 18:19)

He brought me up also out of an horrible pit, out of the miry clay, and set my feet upon a rock, and established my goings. (Psalm 40:2)

68. Beyond Limitation

Today, I speak over my life and my household that the power in the blood of the everlasting covenant speaks mercy concerning us.

God shows me the goodness of His person, and I am forgiven and not forsaken. The strength of His love has redeemed me, and I am saved to serve. My life is precious in His eyes, and I am protected by His great grace. No weapon fashioned or formed against me shall prosper, every tongue that rises against me in judgment I rebuke, and nothing is against me. I am blessed beyond the curse and lifted beyond the limitations of my humanity. When I partake of the divine nature, the light of the presence of the Lord leads me into an abundant place. I am established in the wealthy place; I prosper and profit in righteousness. The spirit of the Lord jet-propels me above every barrier, the chains of limitation are broken, and I experience the ceaseless flow of the spirit of holiness. I have peace with God, and my ways are pleasing unto Him. The Lord is my salvation, and men honor me. I am healed, and I walk in health, for the power of the Lords broken body breaks the yoke of infirmity. The power of sin is destroyed, and death is swallowed up in victory. I belong to God, and I live in the fullness of His love. I reign in life, and I enjoy the pleasures of His right hand forever. Every day is an addition to me. Heaven responds to me, the earth answers to me, and I eat of the good of the land. I am numbered with the strong. The life of God flows through me, and I have dominion as God commanded.

In Jesuss name, I believe and say amen.

Selected Affirmations

I am blessed beyond the curse, and I am lifted beyond the limitations of my humanity.

I am established in the wealthy place.

Suggested Scriptures

And to Jesus the mediator of the new covenant, and to the blood of sprinkling, that speaketh better things than that of Abel. (Hebrews 12:24)

In whom we have redemption through his blood, even the forgiveness of sins. (Colossians 1:14)

Whereby are given unto us exceeding great and precious promises: that by these ye might be partakers of the divine nature, having escaped the corruption that is in the world through lust. (2 Peter 1:4)

And when Jesus saw her, he called her to him, and said unto her, Woman, thou art loosed from thine infirmity. (Luke 13:12)

69. God Rules

Today, I speak over my life and my household that God satisfies us with the bounty of His household and settles us as He has promised.

His faithfulness abides with me, and I am created to fulfill His purpose. God opens doors of opportunities for me, and I am empowered to go through and maximize my moment. Nothing stops me; no man shall stand before me. Darkness becomes as light, and God guides me with His eyes and by the counsel of His will. I will not miss it; I will not miss out. I am a son of God, led by the spirit. I am not dull of hearing, and I have the vision of an eagle. I am directed into greener pastures; I will not suffer. The era of confusion in my life has come to an end. I am not stranded, for God leads the way and I follow. He is my shepherd, and I am the sheep of His pasture. I have wisdom. My life is governed by the Creator of the universe; all things work together for my own good, and I am the called of God according to His purpose. Heaven and earth are in alignment for the fulfillment of my destiny; nothing is against me, and God loves me. The glory of God radiates on my life. I sow and reap a bountiful harvest; I know no loss, for I am a fruitful vine and bring forth my fruit in all seasons. My soil is watered by the streams of the river of life. The leaves of my tree are for the healing of the nations. I am established in Gods presence. I rise to the top, break every barrier, and scale every wall of limitation; I am lifted in righteousness. I have access to the throne of grace by the power in the blood of the eternal covenant. God hears and answers me when I pray. I am favored.

In Jesuss name, I believe and say amen.

Selected Affirmations

The era of confusion in my life has come to an end.

Darkness becomes as light, and God guides me with His eyes and by the counsel of His will.

Suggested Scriptures

But the God of all grace, who hath called us unto his eternal glory by Christ Jesus, after that ye have suffered a while, make you perfect, stablish, strengthen, settle you. (1 Peter 5:10)

And to the angel of the church in Philadelphia write; These things saith he that is holy, he that is true, he that hath the key of David, he that openeth, and no man shutteth; and shutteth, and no man openeth. (Revelation 3:7)

In thee, O Lord, do I put my trust: let me never be put to confusion. (Psalm 71:1)

And he shall be like a tree planted by the rivers of water, that bringeth forth his fruit in his season; his leaf also shall not wither; and whatsoever he doeth shall prosper. (Psalm 1:3)

70. Victory

Today, I speak over my life and my household that the Lord arises for us and that His enemies are scattered.

God fights all my battles, and I hold my peace, so I am triumphant in all the battles of life. God is on my side, He is still with me, and He has not left me. I rejoice in His presence; I have fullness of joy, the hills melt like wax before me, and the mountains skip like rams. Every fallow ground is tilled up, the winding road is made straight, and I am edified by the grace of the Lord. God keeps me, so I dwell in safety. My gifts and callings find divine expression, and I fulfill my purpose; I have an understanding of my vision in God. Creation supports my cause, heaven approves my progress, and I have favor with God. God has disapproved every attempt to subvert my glorious destiny. My life is protected, and my path is illuminated; there is no darkness on my way. I have the mind of Christ, for I am a son of God by the spirit of adoption and a partaker of the divine nature. I have dominion as a right and privilege of the heirs of salvation, and good things must happen to me. The spirit of God motivates me, and the breath of the Almighty inspires me. I increase in the revelation of God in Christ Jesus. I discover the path to establishment and a victorious life in God, so my steps are steady and sure. God is my help, and He gives His angels charge over me. He is my fortress, my defense and my righteousness; my head is covered in the day of battle. God is there for me always, so nothing is impossible for me. My life is insured by His blood.

In Jesuss name, I believe and say amen.

Selected Affirmations

God fights all my battles, and I hold my peace, so I am triumphant in all the battles of life.

Creation supports my cause, heaven approves my progress, and I have favor with God. God has disapproved every attempt to subvert my glorious destiny.

Suggested Scriptures

Let God arise, let his enemies be scattered: let them also that hate him flee before him. (Psalm 68:1)

Thou wilt shew me the path of life: in thy presence is fullness of joy; at thy right hand there are pleasures for evermore. (Psalm 16:11)

To subvert a man in his cause, the Lord approveth not. (Lamentations 3:36)

Thou madest him to have dominion over the works of thy hands; thou hast put all things under his feet. (Psalm 8:6)

71. Eternal Glory

Today, I speak over my life and my household that we are not forsaken and shall not beg for bread.

God remembers me for good and shows me mercy wherever I go. I am kept in safety and jealously guarded as the apple of His eye. I am surrounded by His loving kindness that is better than life itself. The angels of God watch over every step I take, and my feet are protected, never to be dashed against the stone. Every rock of offence is avoided, and I walk with a clear conscience, my mind staying on Him. My confidence is in the Lord my God; He is my fortress, and I am never shaken. I shall not see shame, for disgrace is far from me and I am delivered from all affliction. God is with me; I am a candidate of His eternal glory, and I have joy everlasting. My hope is eternal. I am guarded with the spirit of might in my inward man, and I can do all things through Christ, who strengthens me. This God is my God forever; He will be my guide from now even till the end. The purpose of the Lord is fulfilled in my life; I have a clearer vision of a great destiny in God by the revelation knowledge of God, and nothing stops me from seeking God. My ways are prepared before the Lord. I am a champion, for the power of God flows through me. I am empowered by the spirit of the Lord, and the power of Holiness separates me from the rest. I achieve uncommon results. I am stronger than the tests and challenges of life; I am stronger than the battles before me. My faith endures the trial, and I rise above the odds and shine like the star in the midst of the darkness. I have the keys of David; God keeps His covenant with me. It is my month of remembrance. God has not forsaken me. It is my turn to laugh, my time of rejoicing. Nothing can stop my praise. It is harvest time; my barn is full, and my storehouses abound in the goodness of Gods treasures. I am a blessing to Gods creation.

In Jesuss name, I believe and say amen.

Selected Affirmations

I am a candidate of His eternal glory, and I have joy everlasting. My hope is eternal.

Suggested Scriptures

I have been young, and now am old; yet have I not seen the righteous forsaken, nor his seed begging bread. (Psalm 37:25)

For thus saith the Lord of hosts; After the glory hath he sent me unto the nations which spoiled you: for he that toucheth you toucheth the apple of his eye. (Zechariah 2:8)

That he would grant you, according to the riches of his glory, to be strengthened with might by his Spirit in the inner man. (Ephesians 3:16)

That the trial of your faith, being much more precious than of gold that perisheth, though it be tried with fire, might be found unto praise and honour and glory at the appearing of Jesus Christ. (1 Peter 1:7)

72. My Hedge of Protection

Today, I speak over my life and my household that God is our rock and hiding place.

He is my fortress and my hedge of protection, and I am secure and safe from the insurrection of the enemy. God is the shield around me; God is my glory and the lifter of my head. My heart rejoices in the Lord at all times, for He is my confidence and my armor in the midst of battle. God is my tower of strength, so my arms bend bows of steel. God destroys every giant set to intimidate my life. My purpose is intact, my vision renewed. I am assisted by God for the days ahead, heaven supports my cause, and I am a success. God has me covered. I am marvelously helped, for I have access to the presence of the Lord by the blood of the everlasting covenant. God hears me when I call, and He is at peace with me. I am not downcast, for God is for me, and nothing and no one can be against me. It is my season of diverse promotion, divine elevation, and supernatural establishment. It is my time of abundant harvest. God rewards me according to His grace and mercy. As I go forward, God exceeds my expectation, and I have more than I bargained for. God is magnified in my life, and I am loved perfectly. Fear is destroyed; I am not a slave to fear, for I have the spirit of love, power, and a sound mind. I am created in the image and the likeness of God. My sins are forgiven, and I am redeemed by the blood of the cross. I am saved to serve, and I do not serve in vain. God is my exceedingly great reward. The works of my hands prosper. My barn is full, and my storehouses abound in the goodness of Gods treasures. I am a blessing to Gods creation.

In Jesuss name, I believe and say amen.

Selected Affirmations

I have access to the presence of the Lord by the blood of the everlasting covenant.

I am secure and safe from the insurrection of the enemy. God is the shield around me, my glory, and the lifter of my head.

Suggested Scriptures

Thou art my hiding place; thou shalt preserve me from trouble; thou shalt compass me about with songs of deliverance. Selah. (Psalm 32:7)

For thou art my rock and my fortress; therefore for thy names sake lead me, and guide me. (Psalm 31:3)

So David prevailed over the Philistine with a sling and with a stone, and smote the Philistine, and slew him; but there was no sword in the hand of David. (1 Samuel 17:50)

The Lord is far from the wicked: but he heareth the prayer of the righteous. (Proverbs 15:29)

73. Life

Today, I speak over my life and my household that God breathes on us afresh and that the wisdom of God inspires us anew.

Gods purpose is established over my life, and the peace of God garrisons my heart. God makes a way for me, and I have unlimited access into the throne room of heaven; angels obey the word of life in my mouth. I have life abundant and life eternal; I have the life of Christ flowing in me, so I live and shall not die. I have found the path of purpose; I have the revelation of Gods vision for my life. This is my appointed time, it will surely come to pass, and the darkness is dismissed by the brightness of the light of Gods word. I see my way clear, for my eyes see Gods exceedingly high expectation of my life. I am a living witness to the attainment of destiny; creation announces the reality of Gods promises to me. I got it right, and God smiles at me. The glory of God evolves over my life. God lifts me to where He has determined from before the foundations of the world. God is good to me, I have found favor, and things work out for me. I delight myself in the Lord, and I have the desires of my heart. God hears me when I call, and I have received the mercy of the Lord. I am comforted. Every mountain has become a plain before me; the commandment for my elevation has been made. Gods righteous instruction for my promotion has been made, and the earth is in full cooperation with the divine acclaim and heavenly proclamation. I am lifted accordingly, I am promoted suddenly, and my constant and consistent elevation is established for eternity. God is my exceedingly great reward. The works of my hands prosper; my barn is full, and my storehouses abound in the goodness of Gods treasures. I am a blessing to Gods creation.

In Jesuss name, I believe and say amen.

Selected Affirmations

I live and shall not die. I have found the path of purpose; I have the revelation of Gods vision for my life.

My eyes see Gods exceedingly high expectation of my life. I am a living witness to the attainment of destiny.

Suggested Scriptures

And when he had said this, he breathed on them, and saith unto them, Receive ye the Holy Ghost. (John 20:22)

And the peace of God, which passeth all understanding, shall keep your hearts and minds through Christ Jesus. (Philippians 4:7)

But his delight is in the law of the Lord; and in his law doth he meditate day and night. (Psalm 1:2)

And suddenly there was a great earthquake, so that the foundations of the prison were shaken: and immediately all the doors were opened, and every ones bands were loosed. (Acts 16:26)

74. Breaking Forth

Today, I speak over my life and my household that God watches over us continually.

The eyes of the Lord remain upon me at all times. God remembers me for good, and I am called up suddenly to be promoted, my life experiences a positive change, and my name is mentioned for honor. I change places, but God has not forgotten me, and His face is not hidden from me. I am the beloved of the Lord, and the power of His mercy and love are stronger in my life. God arises for my help, and I am redeemed for His mercys sake. I am not stranded; God leads me in the way, and I will not go astray with the eyes of the Lord upon me. I am guided by the light of His presence; the countenance of the Lord brightens my path, and I prosper in all I do. I have peace like a river, I abound in righteousness like the waves of the sea, my seed are as the sand, and the offspring of my bowels cover the earth. I remain relevant to Gods scheme on earth, and my name abides continually unto eternity. My borders are enlarged, the curtains of my habitation are stretched, my cords are lengthened, and my stakes are strengthened, I break forth in all directions, and my seed inherit the promises of God and rebuild desolate cities. Mountains depart, hills are removed, and the Lords kindness abides with me forever, for His covenant of peace is still in place over my life. I am established in righteousness and far from oppression. I am afraid of nothing; terror shall not come near me. My heritage is maintained in the Lord, and my place is established in Him. Gods faithfulness sustains me through this season, and I am protected by the power of His right hand. It is my time, so its my turn. My light shines like the brightness of the sun at midday; kings come to the brightness of my rising, and the darkness is dispelled at the power of the light of Gods presence. God loves me. My barn is full, and my storehouses abound in the goodness of Gods treasures. I am a blessing to Gods creation.

In Jesuss name, I believe and say amen.

Selected Affirmations

I break forth in all directions; my seed inherit the promises of God and rebuild desolate cities. Mountains depart, hills are removed, and the Lords kindness abides with me forever.

Suggested Scriptures

Then said the Lord unto me, Thou hast well seen: for I will hasten my word to perform it. (Jeremiah 1:12)

And he remembered for them his covenant, and repented according to the multitude of his mercies. (Psalm 106:45)

O that thou hadst hearkened to my commandments! then had thy peace been as a river, and thy righteousness as the waves of the sea. (Isaiah 48:18)

For thou shalt break forth on the right hand and on the left; and thy seed shall inherit the Gentiles, and make the desolate cities to be inhabited. (Isaiah 54:3)

75. Blessings Reloaded

Today, I speak over my life and my household that the grace of new beginnings rests upon us and that God settles all that concerns us.

As I move into my season of divine restoration, God brings it all back. I do not return empty, for God has commanded the reloading of my storehouses. I have abundance, the enemy has been caught, and heaven insists on a seven-fold repayment. God sends me help, so I have favor from quarters unexpected. Gods mighty hand has established me, so nothing shall be difficult for me. All things are possible for me, for I am a believer. The grace of God distinguishes me. It is evident that I am loved by God, for I break through on all sides and doors open for me of their own accord. Creation bears a witness of Gods gifts and calling over my life. I am a solution provider, a blessing to Gods creation, and the fulfillment of Gods purpose. I have the revelation of Gods plan for my life. The power and the zeal of God enable me in the pursuit of my vision, so I cannot fail. I achieve my vision, for the zeal of the Lord makes it a possibility and nothing stops me. My helpers find me; I have angelic support and am empowered by the Holy Spirit. I have my eyes on my goal. I pursue my dreams doggedly and consistently. I am a success, for God leads me and His eyes guide me into all truth. My works endure, I lose nothing, and destruction is far from me. It is my turn and my time. Every good thing must happen to me; it is my due season. Nothing pertaining to life and godliness is held back from me; its my new season, the dawn of a new day. I see the goodness of God in the land of the living. My barn is full, and my storehouses abound in the goodness of Gods treasures. I am a blessing to Gods creation.

In Jesuss name, I believe and say amen.

Selected Affirmations

I have abundance, the enemy has been caught, and heaven insists on a seven-fold repayment.

The power and the zeal of God enable me in the pursuit of my vision, so I cannot fail. I achieve my vision, and the zeal of the Lord makes it a possibility.

Suggested Scriptures

This month shall be unto you the beginning of months: it shall be the first month of the year to you. (Exodus 12:2)

Then thou shalt see, and flow together, and thine heart shall fear, and be enlarged; because the abundance of the sea shall be converted unto thee, the forces of the Gentiles shall come unto thee. (Isaiah 60:5)

Men do not despise a thief, if he steal to satisfy his soul when he is hungry;But if he be found, he shall restore sevenfold; he shall give all the substance of his house. (Proverbs 6:30)

When they were past the first and the second ward, they came unto the iron gate that leadeth unto the city; which opened to them of his own accord: and they went out, and passed on through one street; and forthwith the angel departed from him. (Acts 12:10)

76. Breaking the Chains of Mediocrity

Today, I speak over my life and my household that God comes through for us and that the Almighty delivers us speedily.

Nothing stands between me and my God-ordained destiny; my purpose is revealed, and the light of Gods countenance shines upon my path. I am not confused, for I have divine direction. I do not grope in the dark, for my steps are flooded with the light of Gods word. The chains of mediocrity are broken, and I am established in the power of Gods perfect will for my life. The heavy basket of stagnancy is lifted off my shoulders, and I break forth into the fulfillment of Gods amazing promises. Heaven proclaims my emancipation; my release has been announced, and I go forward to do Gods will as it written in the volume of the book concerning me. My cause is just, for the Lord does not approve any plan to subvert my destiny. God takes care of me and mine. I am not a slave to fear, for God loves me ever so perfectly. The God of glory is magnified in my life. The heavens are opened up to me, and the clouds over me are heavy; I hear the sound of abundance-bearing rain. The drought is over, and the rains of blessing are poured out over me in a deluge. It is harvest time, and the threshing floor is full of wheat and grain. I have peace on all sides, for God has comforted me again; God has shown me mercy, and the Son of righteousness is risen over me with healing in His wings. The blood speaks for me, so I have access to the throne room of grace. Gods will cannot deny me. I am an asset to creation. Nothing pertaining to life and godliness is held back from me, and I see the goodness of God in the land of the living. My barn is full, and my storehouses abound in the goodness of Gods treasures. I am a blessing to Gods creation.

In Jesuss name, I believe and say amen.

Selected Affirmations

Nothing stands between me and my God-ordained destiny; my purpose is revealed, and the light of Gods countenance shines upon my path.

Suggested Scriptures

Bow down thine ear to me; deliver me speedily: be thou my strong rock, for an house of defence to save me. (Psalm 31:2)

After that he put his hands again upon his eyes, and made him look up: and he was restored, and saw every man clearly. (Mark 8:25)

For thou shalt break forth on the right hand and on the left; and thy seed shall inherit the Gentiles, and make the desolate cities to be inhabited. (Isaiah 54:3)

And Elijah said unto Ahab, Get thee up, eat and drink; for there is a sound of abundance of rain. (1 Kings 18:41)

77. I Believe In God

Today, I speak over my life and my household that God has provided better things for us and is keeping us perfect without blame.

My faith delivers, and I trust completely in the immutable word of God. I overcome the world, for my faith cannot fail. Gods word comes to pass in my life. I am who God says I am; every man be a liar, but Gods word is the truth. My future is sustained by the same word that created the heaven and earth. Now I know all things work together for my good, and I am loved by God and called according to His purpose. I am established in His perfect will. I am justified, I am accepted in the beloved, and I have great faith. My ways are pleasing unto God, and I am forgiven; my enemies submit to me, for they are at peace with me. I am the righteousness of God in Christ. I have the witness of a good report. I am exempt from all evil that is common to man. I am in agreement with God, having been reconciled with Him; God walks with me. My days are secured in Him, and my life is framed by the word of the Lord. God is my shield and my exceedingly great reward. He rewards me. God is at work in me, to will and make me do His good pleasure. The day of His power is upon me. I walk before God, and I am blameless. My mouth is satisfied with the goodness of His presence. I have the fullness of joy, and I see the abundance of His right hand eternally. I am an heir of righteousness by faith; Gods promises to me find fulfillment. I soar above every wind of distraction, I keep my eyes on the prize, and I am focused on the mark; my life remains on track. I am passionately consumed by the zeal of the Lord. I shall deliver on my purpose, and my lifes vision will be established. My ways prosper before the Lord. I am victorious, and success is attracted to me. My barn is full, and my storehouses abound in the goodness of Gods treasures. I am a blessing to Gods creation.

In Jesuss name, I believe and say amen.

My future is sustained by the same word that created the heaven and earth. Now I know all things work together for my good.

I am an heir of righteousness by faith; Gods promises to me find fulfilment.

I soar above every wind of distraction, I keep my eyes on the prize, and I am focused on the mark; my life remains on track.

Suggested Scriptures

God having provided some better thing for us, that they without us should not be made perfect. (Hebrews 11:40)

I laid me down and slept; I awaked; for the Lord sustained me. (Psalm 3:5)

When a mans ways please the Lord, he maketh even his enemies to be at peace with him. (Proverbs 16:7)

And if ye be Christs, then are ye Abrahams seed, and heirs according to the promise. (Galatians 3:29)

78. Marked and Lifted

Today, I speak over my life and my household that we are precious in the eyes of the Lord and that He upholds us with the strength of His righteous right hand.

The Lord is mindful of me; I am not forsaken. My life is constantly before Him; I am not forgotten. God remembers me for good, and His word has gone out before me that I must prosper in all my ways. He has given His command, so help finds me and I have divine assistance and angelic support. Gods eyes lead me as I progress in life, and I am kept on the path of righteousness for His names sake. My heart finds rest in God alone. My bones are revived, and resurrection power is at work in me. My destiny is intact. Purpose is fulfilled in my life. God did not overlook me; everything is working together for my own good. I have been marked for uplifting. God has pulled me up, so I am raised and have been promoted. It is my season of visitation. God is on my side. Mercy meets me, favor follows me, I have received the call to comfort, and it is well with me always. The storm is over, and the peace of the Lord is my portion. I have a new beginning. I break through on all fronts, and I break forth on all sides. Men seek my goodness; I am an amazement to many. I was created a sign and a wonder. Creation is blessed by my sojourn, and the world is better by the impact of my presence. I am a positive influence on humanity. I am a blessing to mankind. My barn is full, and my storehouses abound in the goodness of Gods treasures. I am a blessing to Gods creation.

In Jesuss name, I believe and say amen.

SELECTED AFFIRMATIONS

Gods eyes lead me as I progress in life.

God has pulled me up. I am raised, and I have been promoted.

SUGGESTED SCRIPTURES

Fear thou not; for I am with thee: be not dismayed; for I am thy God: I will strengthen thee; yea, I will help thee; yea, I will uphold thee with the right hand of my righteousness. (Isaiah 41:10)

Since thou wast precious in my sight, thou hast been honourable, and I have loved thee: therefore will I give men for thee, and people for thy life. (Isaiah 43:4)

Think upon me, my God, for good, according to all that I have done for this people. (Nehemiah 5:19)

He maketh the storm a calm, so that the waves thereof are still. (Psalm 107:29)

79. Appointed for the Top

Today, I speak over my life and my household that God watches over us to keep us safe.

I am protected as I dwell securely under the shadow of His wings; God is my strong tower and my guide. I will not miss the mark; the voice of the Lord guides me along the way, and I am attentive to the prompting of the spirit of the living God. I am led by God. I am a child of God; He died for my sins, and Hes alive for my justification. I am created for purpose, I am the zenith of Gods creation, and I am a dominant force in my generation. I am appointed for destiny. God has me covered, and creation awaits my manifestation as a son of God. I am prepared for greatness. My time has come; its my appointed time, and doors open for me, for God remembers me for good. I am settled for life and repositioned for power. God delights in my life. I see Gods faithfulness upon my life, for the finger of God is at work in my life. Gods purpose is stretched out over my life; there is no going back. The will of God is done, and the Kings dominion is established in my life. I prosper in all my endeavors. Angels watch over me, my enemies bow down to me, God honors me, and men favor me. My future is settled in God, and my testimony is in place. I am not limited in life, for I am a prince of God. I am a positive influence on humanity. I am a blessing to mankind. My barn is full, and my storehouses abound in the goodness of Gods treasures. I am a blessing to Gods creation.

In Jesuss name, I believe and say amen.

Selected Affirmations

The Kings dominion is established in my life. I prosper in all my endeavors. Angels watch over me, my enemies bow down to me, God honors me, and men favor me.

Suggested Scriptures

He shall cover thee with his feathers, and under his wings shalt thou trust: his truth shall be thy shield and buckler. (Psalm 91:4)

Who was delivered for our offences, and was raised again for our justification. (Romans 4:25)

And thine ears shall hear a word behind thee, saying, This is the way, walk ye in it, when ye turn to the right hand, and when ye turn to the left. (Isaiah 30:21)

Then the magicians said unto Pharaoh, This is the finger of God: and Pharaohs heart was hardened, and he hearkened not unto them; as the Lord had said. (Exodus 8:19)

80. The Yoke Is Broken

Today, I speak over my life and my household that the power of the Almighty sees us through and that the grace of the Lord flows freely toward us.

As I enter into my season of divine possibilities, it is my turn for Gods special touch. My time is now, and my set time has come. God keeps His appointment with me; my wait is over, and I have been called in. My teary eyes are wiped clean, and I have joy unspeakable. I am full of glory, and people rejoice with me. God has turned things around for me. I have not waited in vain; life has a new meaning, and the Prince of Peace has given a peaceful response. I found a new life in Him, and He has remembered me and fulfilled His promises to me. The vicious cycle has been broken, and the yoke of delay has been shattered; God has vindicated me by His mercy, and heaven favors me. The righteousness of the Lord has delivered me, for the Lord delights in the joy of His own. I have seen the Lords goodness; the Lord is compassionate toward me, and God is faithful to me. He has given me as a light to the people of the world and made me a proof of His saving grace. Kings shall see me arise, princes also shall worship because God has chosen me. Today is the day of salvation. God helps me, preserves me, and has shown me as a beacon of light for the sake of His covenant to establish the earth and to inherit the desolate places. I am not forgotten; God has not forsaken me. God contends with my contenders and has defeated all my foes. I am victorious in Him. I am a blessing to mankind. My barn is full, and my storehouses abound in the goodness of Gods treasures. I am a blessing to Gods creation.

In Jesus name, I believe and say amen.

Selected Affirmations

The vicious cycle has been broken, and the yoke of delay has been shattered; God has vindicated me by His mercy, and heaven favors me.

Today is the day of salvation. God helps me, preserves me, and has shown me as a beacon of light for the sake of His covenant to establish the earth and to inherit the desolate places.

Suggested Scriptures

And God is able to make all grace abound toward you; that ye, always having all sufficiency in all things, may abound to every good work. (2 Corinthians 9:8)

Then I will give you rain in due season, and the land shall yield her increase, and the trees of the field shall yield their fruit. (Leviticus 26:4)

Therefore we are buried with him by baptism into death: that like as Christ was raised up from the dead by the glory of the Father, even so we also should walk in newness of life. (Romans 6:4)

But thus saith the Lord, Even the captives of the mighty shall be taken away, and the prey of the terrible shall be delivered: for I will contend with him that contendeth with thee, and I will save thy children. (Isaiah 49:25)

81. Rejoice in the Lord

Today, I speak over my life and my household that God restores all we have lost and revives us in the midst of our days.

I get all back, for God commands divine restoration to me, and the enemy pays back seven times. The word of God comes to pass in my life, for the word has found me out. I am free, liberated from the shackles of delay and denial. My hands are lifted in perpetual praise to my King as I rejoice in the presence of my Lord. Joy swallows every appearance of sorrow, for I live, I am alive, I have life, I am blessed with eternal life, I have life abundant, and I have the breath of God in me. I am selected to do good works, and my life and destiny are on course. I am not distracted; my eyes are focused, set on my goal. God leads me into the fullness of His plan and purpose for my life, and I get the full supply of the spirit of God. Heaven supports my bidding, and the angelic hosts help me out. I have the victory, my life radiates Gods glory, and the light of His presence blazes through every representation of darkness. I walk in light, not in frustration, and I am settled for life. God has blessed me with all things that pertain to life and godliness in Christ Jesus. I live life on purpose. God satisfies the longing of my soul, so I do not lack. It is well with me. I walk in wisdom, grace, peace, and the counsel of Gods spirit. God has provided for me. My heart is at rest, and I enter into a new time and season of my life. As I break forth in all areas of my life, I see the goodness of God in the land of the living. My barn is full, and my storehouses abound in the goodness of Gods treasures. I am a blessing to Gods creation.

In Jesuss name, I believe and say amen.

SELECTED AFFIRMATIONS

I rejoice in the presence of my Lord. Joy swallows every appearance of sorrow.

I walk in light, not in frustration, and I am settled for life. I walk in wisdom, grace, peace, and the counsel of Gods spirit.

SUGGESTED SCRIPTURES

For thus saith the high and lofty One that inhabiteth eternity, whose name is Holy; I dwell in the high and holy place, with him also that is of a contrite and humble spirit, to revive the spirit of the humble, and to revive the heart of the contrite ones. (Isaiah 57:15)

And the king answered and said unto the man of God, Intreat now the face of the Lord thy God, and pray for me, that my hand may be restored me again. And the man of God besought the Lord, and the kings hand was restored him again, and became as it was before. (1 Kings 13:6)

The thief cometh not, but for to steal, and to kill, and to destroy: I am come that they might have life, and that they might have it more abundantly. (John 10:10)

For I know that this shall turn to my salvation through your prayer, and the supply of the Spirit of Jesus Christ. (Philippians 1:19)

82. All Things Are New

Today, I speak over my life and my household that God makes our mountain rise higher and that our lives emerge gloriously.

I press toward the mark of the high calling in Christ Jesus. I attain the purpose that God created me for and that is revealed to me. Nothing prevents the manifestation of divine destiny in my life. I am duly lifted by the amazing grace of a loving God. My work is directed in truth, and Gods everlasting covenant is in force over my life. I am clothed in the garments of salvation; He has covered me with the robe of righteousness. The wilderness and solitary places are glad for me, and the desert places rejoice over me. I am a repairer of the breach, a rebuilder of ancient desolation; the creative power of the Lord my God is at work through me, and the resurrection power of the Lord is alive in me. I live again, I remain in health, I am protected, and I rest secure in the goodness of my God. My hands are strengthened, and my knees find strength to stand. I am strong, for God avenges me of my enemies. Every parched land becomes a pool; every thirsty land springs forth water. The drought is over, and the siege is broken. My soul finds rest in God alone. The dry bones are revived, and God gives me the victory. God holds my hands and leads me with His eyes. The former things are passed, and He does a new thing in my life. Darkness is as light before me, and God makes the crooked places straight. I am raised in righteousness, and my ways are prepared before the Lord. God is my help and my defense, my shield and a mighty fortress. I am delivered from the striving of the tongue and saved from the pride of man. Shame and disgrace are far from me. I am a person of honor, mercy, and grace. I am created for favor, and success is attracted to me. He is my peace, and I am reconciled to Him by the blood of the lamb. My storehouses abound in the goodness of Gods treasures. I am a blessing to Gods creation.

In Jesus name, I believe and say amen.

Selected Affirmations

I am clothed in the garments of salvation; He has covered me with the robe of righteousness. The wilderness and solitary places are glad for me; the desert places rejoice for me. I am a repairer of the breach, a rebuilder of ancient desolation.

Darkness is as light before me, and God makes the crooked places straight.

Suggested Scriptures

Lord, by thy favour thou hast made my mountain to stand strong: thou didst hide thy face, and I was troubled. (Psalm 30:7)

I press toward the mark for the prize of the high calling of God in Christ Jesus. (Philippians 3:14)

Therefore now let your hands be strengthened, and be ye valiant: for your master Saul is dead, and also the house of Judah have anointed me king over them. (2 Samuel 2:7)

And the parched ground shall become a pool, and the thirsty land springs of water: in the habitation of dragons, where each lay, shall be grass with reeds and rushes. (Isaiah 35:7)

83. My Confidence

Today, I speak over my life and my household that God sends help our way and that heaven supports us.

I do not lack provision, for God is my source, so I have the fullness of the storehouses of the King of heaven according to His riches in glory. Angels are watching over me, my steps are ordered by God, and the outcome of my life is determined by Gods faithfulness. I have grace to run the race set before me, and I will end well. I am highly favored, and God keeps me. My covenant with God is in place; He watches over His word on my life to bring it to pass. This is the source of my confidence: God hears and answers my prayers, and I have not cried out to Him in vain. I break through on every side. I experience open doors in every area of my life. I am set free to become the best in life; destiny beckons, purpose calls, and Gods grace is poured out to me. I am upheld by the hand of the Lord, the power of the Holy Spirit is upon me, and the power of God overshadows me. There is no impossibility with me. I step out of insignificance and move forward into Gods purpose. This is my time; it is my turn. People rejoice with me, sorrow is defeated, I have joy like the ceaseless flow of a river, and delay is destroyed. I enter into my season of divine fulfillment, and light floods my path. I see through every bout of frustration, and my way is clear, for I have wisdom. The word of the Lord heals me, the balm of Gilead is poured out over me, and I walk in divine healing. I am created for signs and wonders. I walk unhindered into the newness of Gods promises to me. It is the day of the Lord, and I have the willingness to become the best in life. The oil of ease establishes me in dominion. I am a child of the King, and I cannot be held down. Limitations and false ceilings are destroyed. I break forth from the breach, and I experience supernatural expansion on all fronts. God has lifted my head above my haters. I am a barrier breaker. My storehouses abound in the goodness of Gods treasures. I am a blessing to Gods creation.

In Jesus name, I believe and say Amen.

SELECTED AFFIRMATIONS

This is the source of my confidence: God hears and answers my prayers, and I have not cried out to Him in vain.

The word of the Lord heals me, the balm of Gilead is poured out over me, and I walk in divine healing.

SUGGESTED SCRIPTURES

Even by the God of thy father, who shall help thee; and by the Almighty, who shall bless thee with blessings of heaven above, blessings of the deep that lieth under, blessings of the breasts, and of the womb. (Genesis 49:25)

Then said the Lord unto me, Thou hast well seen: for I will hasten my word to perform it. (Jeremiah 1:12)

And suddenly there was a great earthquake, so that the foundations of the prison were shaken: and immediately all the doors were opened, and every ones bands were loosed. (Acts 16:26)

And he said, The things which are impossible with men are possible with God. (Luke 18:27)

84. Fruitfulness

Today, I speak over my life and my household that God is at peace with us and has turned to us with favor.

God has granted me the grace of divine restorationnothing broken and nothing missing. I found my peace under the shadow of His wings; I am covered and protected in the hollow of His palms. My adversaries are consumed in the fire of His jealousy and will bear the shame of the heathen. I shoot my branches and yield my fruit in and out of season. God is for me; nothing is against me. My life is tilled and sown. I see increase and bring forth fruit abundantly. God has done better to me than at my beginning; my latter end is better than my past. I possess my possessions; my inheritance is secure. God has pitied me for His names sake. I have been baptized in the sea of Gods mercy, and the voice of the blood of the eternal covenant speaks on my behalf. He sprinkles clean water on me, and I am cleansed, I have a new heart, and God gives me a new spirit. I walk in His statutes, I keep His judgment, and I am obedient to His instructions. I am in line for the miraculous move of His divine power. God has saved me from uncleanness. He called for corn and increased my harvest. The famine is not laid upon me. The fruit of my tree is multiplied, and my fields yield their increase. I am jubilant, and I hear the sound of an abundant rain. I hear the blast of the trumpet. It my season of divine favor. God remembers me for good; it is my turn. It is my time, and the wait is over; God sends me help for destinys sake. I access what has been supernaturally provided for the achievement of my vision. My storehouses abound in the goodness of Gods treasures. I am a blessing to Gods creation.

In Jesuss name, I believe and say amen.

Selected Affirmations

The famine is not laid upon me. The fruit of my tree is multiplied, and my fields yield their increase. I hear the sound of the abundance of rain. I hear the blast of the trumpet. It my season of divine favor.

Suggested Scriptures

Therefore being justified by faith, we have peace with God through our Lord Jesus Christ. (Romans 5:1)

Be merciful unto me, O God, be merciful unto me: for my soul trusteth in thee: yea, in the shadow of thy wings will I make my refuge, until these calamities be overpast. (Psalm 57:1)

And he hath made my mouth like a sharp sword; in the shadow of his hand hath he hid me, and made me a polished shaft; in his quiver hath he hid me. (Isaiah 49:2)

And the children of Israel were fruitful, and increased abundantly, and multiplied, and waxed exceeding mighty; and the land was filled with them. (Exodus 1:7)

85. Qualified by Grace

Today, I speak over my life and my household that God, who has brought us this far, has not abandoned us.

God has neither left nor forsaken me. The power of the Holy Spirit is within me, and the presence of the Lord my God makes the difference in my life. Gods power makes the change; God lifts me above every trial, situation, and circumstance so I am empowered to rise above the spirit at work in the sons of disobedience. The grace of God qualifies me for the best of Gods blessings, and every promise in the book is activated on my behalf on the basis of the finished work of the Lord on the cross of Calvary. I am tremendously covered and marvelously assisted by God, so nothing is impossible for me. My helpers seek me out. I am accepted in the beloved, God turned things around for me; now nothing is against me, everything is working in my favor, and I have the joy of the Lord. I am strengthened by the power of the spirit in my inward man. I can do all things through Christ, for now I have the victory in Him. Heaven fights for and supports my cause, so I cannot be subverted. I am alive to and a recipient of Gods great mercy, and I have found grace to help at the time of need. God has not put more on me than I can bear. He is my door and way of escape. He is for me. He is my glory and the One who lifts my head. God has shown me the path of life, and He has healed me and restored me. I have peace, and I am led into the pleasures of His right hand. He has given me an everlasting inheritance in Him. My name and posterity shall not be cut off. I am joyful in His presence, for my sacrifices and offerings are accepted. God sends me help for destinys sake. I access what has been supernaturally provided for the achievement of my vision. My storehouses abound in the goodness of Gods treasures. I am a blessing to Gods creation.

In Jesuss name, I believe and say Amen.

Selected Affirmations

The power of the Holy Spirit is within me, and the presence of the Lord my God makes the difference in my life.

The grace of God qualifies me for the best of Gods blessings; every promise in the book is activated on my behalf on the basis of the finished work of the Lord on the cross of Calvary.

Suggested Scriptures

Be strong and of a good courage, fear not, nor be afraid of them: for the Lord thy God, he it is that doth go with thee; he will not fail thee, nor forsake thee. (Deuteronomy 31:6)

The Lord God of your fathers make you a thousand times so many more as ye are, and bless you, as he hath promised you! (Deuteronomy 1:11)

When Jesus therefore had received the vinegar, he said, It is finished: and he bowed his head, and gave up the ghost. (John 19:30)

But thou, O Lord, art a shield for me; my glory, and the lifter up of mine head. (Psalm 3:3)

86. Divine Acceleration

Today, I speak over my life and my household that God approves my promotion.

I am set up for a sudden miracle. The shout of my praise is ceaseless. My joy and rejoicing are endless. I receive beauty for ashes. I have a double portion for my trouble and the garment of praise for the spirit of heaviness. Things begin to look up for me again, and the bitterness of frustration becomes a thing of the past. Ways open up to me, and I pass through to another level victoriously. I am delivered from endless labor to unprecedented favor. My light is come, and I arise and shine. The glory of God descends heavily upon me. I make the change. I am set apart for a life of distinction. I am elevated higher than every human expectation. Grace separates me from averageness, and Gods righteous right hand lifts me above all incidents of mediocrity. I see my way clear and walk straight into my promise, for the pathway to destinys shore is free. I have divine acceleration. I am guided by the power of the spirit, and I walk through unhindered. I activate the grace for an impactful life and an enviable future. I navigate life with ease. I am born a sign, and I daily walk in the miraculous. Things happen for me. Good things happen to me. The lines fall for me in pleasant places always. I have a Godly heritage, so nothing makes me afraid. God loves me perfectly, so I am protected. God provides for me. God is my source. God is my peace. Nothing is missing, nothing broken. I am a wonder to creation, an amazement to the world. Gods faithfulness and kindness is guaranteed to my eternal generation by divine covenant. I live life unhindered. I have mercy without limit, for I am blood bought and am spirit led. I am Gods love. I am jealously guarded. I have the victory. I am a solution provider. I have a part with the mighty, and my lot is with the strong. Im blessed before and above the curse. I belong to the triumphant company.

In Jesuss name, I believe and say amen.

Selected Affirmations

Things begin to look up for me again, and the bitterness of frustration becomes a thing of the past. The way opens up to me, and I pass through to another level victoriously.

Grace separates me from averageness, and Gods righteous right hand lifts me above all incidents of mediocrity.

Suggested Scriptures

Then the king promoted Shadrach, Meshach, and Abednego, in the province of Babylon. (Daniel 3:30)

And suddenly there was a great earthquake, so that the foundations of the prison were shaken: and immediately all the doors were opened, and every ones bands were loosed. (Acts 16:26)

But lift thou up thy rod, and stretch out thine hand over the sea, and divide it: and the children of Israel shall go on dry ground through the midst of the sea. (Exodus 14:16)

The lines are fallen unto me in pleasant places; yea, I have a goodly heritage. (Psalm 16:6)

87. Praise for a Raise

Today, I speak over my life and my household that my praise invokes the presence and the power of the Lord and that His mighty right hand is stretched out to my rescue.

God is my support and my fortress. My pain dissolves at the sound of my praise. I am strengthened by the spirit of might in my inward man. Light shines upon my path so I see my way through. Frustration ends today. Confusion ceases today. God turns my pain into power, and the darkness has become light. My expectation is fulfilled. It is the dawn of a new day for me. My new season starts *now*. My praise secures a raise for me. I am elevated; I am not restrained anymore. My progress in life is sustained and unrestricted. I go forward unrestrained, and my movement upward is limitless. My shout of praise breaks every barrier and shatters every glass ceiling over every area of my life. I live my life like there is no box; I cannot be held down. I run through troops and leap over walls. I am delivered by grace, and I prosper by favor. I have the oil of ease from this day. Success is attracted to me, and struggle is far from me. I am victorious in life; I am a conqueror, I am triumphant, and I am established in dominion. God is pleased with me. My destiny helpers locate me, and I am marvelously helped. I am completely healed. I have divine assistance. Good things happen to me on a daily basis. My testimony is endless. My praise is ceaseless. God hears me, and I am blessed. My shout of hallelujah has challenged the devil, and God is my victory.

In Jesuss name, I believe and say amen.

Selected Affirmations

My pain dissolves at the sound of my praise.

My shout of praise breaks every barrier and shatters every glass ceiling over every area of my life.

Suggested Scriptures

But thou art holy, O thou that inhabitest the praises of Israel. (Psalm 22:3)

Now know I that the Lord saveth his anointed; he will hear him from his holy heaven with the saving strength of his right hand. (Psalm 20:6)

Thy word is a lamp unto my feet, and a light unto my path. (Psalm 119:105)

For by thee I have run through a troop: by my God have I leaped over a wall. (2 Samuel 22:30)

88. Wholeness

Today, I speak over my life and my household that the full benefits of Gods eternal salvation manifests in my life.

I am saved. I am sanctified. I am justified. I am the called of God. I am glorified. I am forgiven. The yoke of sin is broken. I am blood bought. I am cleansed by the washing of water by the word, and I am baptized in the love of the Father. I am healed, and I walk in divine health. The burden of poverty is broken completely over every area of my life. Out of the darkness, the light is called out. I am changed into the fullness of the stature of the Son of God. I have the oil of gladness and ease. I am protected by the angels of God. The elements and creation answer when I call; I am limitless in my reach, and I know no lack. I am a sheep in the pasture of the Lord; I am completely guarded and guided into purpose, and destiny is fulfilled in me. I am connected to the power source. I am a change agent. My story is different. Life and humanity bear witness of my impact upon many generations. My sojourn on the planet is undeniable. I am a solution provider. I am child of consolation, a son of promise, and a person of global prominence and influence. I am wise. I am the light of the world and the salt of the earth. I have access into the mind of God. I walk in possibilities, and nothing is difficult for me. Nothing is missing. Nothing is broken. I have the peace of God that passes all understanding. I am established in wealth; money knows my name. I walk through open doors effortlessly. Its my time, and its my turn. I arise and I shine, and Gods glory is revealed through me. I am a blessing to all I encounter. It is well with me.

In Jesuss name, I believe and say amen.

Selected Affirmations

The yoke of sin is broken. I am blood bought.

I am changed into the fullness of the stature of the Son of God. I have the oil of gladness and ease.

Suggested Scriptures

Before I formed thee in the belly I knew thee; and before thou camest forth out of the womb I sanctified thee, and I ordained thee a prophet unto the nations. (Jeremiah 1:5)

And such were some of you: but ye are washed, but ye are sanctified, but ye are justified in the name of the Lord Jesus, and by the Spirit of our God. (1 Corinthians 6:11)

Till we all come in the unity of the faith, and of the knowledge of the Son of God, unto a perfect man, unto the measure of the stature of the fulness of Christ. (Ephesians 4:13)

Ye are the salt of the earth: but if the salt have lost his savour, wherewith shall it be salted? it is thenceforth good for nothing, but to be cast out, and to be trodden under foot of men. (Matthew 5:13)

89. Divine Honor

Today, I speak over my life and my household that God sees me through this season to a large and prepared place.

I shed the garments of prior prominence and am robed in present power. My life takes a new turn for the better. I am established in the current glory, preserved for this new season, and I am relevant to Gods plan in this generation. I am value added to creation. I remain in dominion. I have received double for my trouble. I have the influence of heaven working for me for a glorious life on earth. My hands remain blessed. My name is mentioned in places that matter, and kings and princes entreat my favor. I remain in honor with the great of the earth, for my head is lifted above those of my peers and foes. I am the preferred and the chosen of the Lord; I am selected above all others. I am favored, and my election is sure. Wealth is stored up for me in abundance while lack is destroyed on the mountain of more than enough. My victory is endless by covenant right. I am drawn out and enthroned. Continental doors of opportunities open up to me, and my gifts make room for me. I have peace like a river and comfort on all sides. God is pleased with me and not mad at me. Good things happen to me always. I am in Christ. The lines have fallen for me in pleasant places. My inheritance is maintained; nothing dispossesses me of the glory reserved for me. God shuts the mouth of my haters. My tongue is filled with His praise eternally, and I am triumphant in Him. I rejoice in the benefits of my salvation. I am a blessed and fulfilled person. It is well with me.

In Jesuss name, I believe and say amen.

Selected Affirmations

I shed the garments of prior prominence and am robed in present power. My life takes a new turn for the better. I am established in the current glory.

God is pleased with me and not mad at me. Good things happen to me always.

Suggested Scriptures

He brought me forth also into a large place; he delivered me, because he delighted in me. (Psalm 18:19)

And I will clothe him with thy robe, and strengthen him with thy girdle, and I will commit thy government into his hand: and he shall be a father to the inhabitants of Jerusalem, and to the house of Judah. (Isaiah 22:21)

Speak ye comfortably to Jerusalem, and cry unto her, that her warfare is accomplished, that her iniquity is pardoned: for she hath received of the Lords hand double for all her sins. (Isaiah 40:2)

For thus saith the Lord, Behold, I will extend peace to her like a river, and the glory of the Gentiles like a flowing stream: then shall ye suck, ye shall be borne upon her sides, and be dandled upon her knees. (Isaiah 66:12)

90. Promise Fulfilled

Lift your hands and say: Today, I declare my testimony is endless, and my praise is ceaseless.

I have joy unspeakable, full of glory. Shouts of victory and triumph resound in my house eternally. It is my season of divine visitation. Everything is changed for the better for me; nothing is the same. I have been lifted, I have been promoted, and I have been healed. I have been elevated. I have been released. God is good to me; I have seen the Lords goodness and witnessed His compassion. I am a recipient of Gods mercy. The yoke of barrenness and unfruitfulness is broken. The chain of protracted singleness is destroyed. My God-ordained spouse and I are united on purpose. Destiny has not eluded me. My future is brighter than my best past. Light covers me, and my path is illuminated. I am free from frustration, confusion, and depression. God is my light and my salvation. Fear is destroyed on the mountain of fulfillment. My mouth is satisfied with good things. God has delivered me. I have an immediate breakthrough and a sudden blessing. Every day from now is an addition. A bespoke miracle is allocated to me. I increase, I prosper, and I live in abundance. I am divinely assisted; the angels bear me on their wings. The blood of the eternal speaks better things about Gods promises for my life. I am established in this season of divine surprises, and God gives me a new story to tell on a daily basis. He brought me from the back to the front just like that. God delivers me. The days of tears and sighing are over, and I move into my season of greatness. Heaven instructs me on my emancipation. Creation favors me. I am set up for global prominence. Its my time. Its my turn. Success is attracted to me. I arise and I shine forever. My shout of hallelujah is endless. I am unstoppable.

In Jesuss name, I believe and say amen.

Selected Affirmations

God is good to me; I have seen the Lords goodness and witnessed His compassion. I am a recipient of Gods mercy.

The chain of protracted singleness is destroyed. My God-ordained spouse and I are united on purpose. Destiny has not eluded me. God gives me a new story to tell on a daily basis.

Suggested Scriptures

Whom having not seen, ye love; in whom, though now ye see him not, yet believing, ye rejoice with joy unspeakable and full of glory. (1 Peter 1:8)

But the Lord was with Joseph, and shewed him mercy, and gave him favour in the sight of the keeper of the prison. (Genesis 39:21)

And to Jesus the mediator of the new covenant, and to the blood of sprinkling, that speaketh better things than that of Abel. (Hebrews 12:24)

A man shall be satisfied with good by the fruit of his mouth: and the recompence of a mans hands shall be rendered unto him. (Proverbs 12:14)

GODFESSIONS

Follow us on;

Facebook: http;/www.facebook.com/godfesions

Instagram: @Godfessions

Website: www.Godfessions.com

Other Books

Godfessions

Godfessions 2

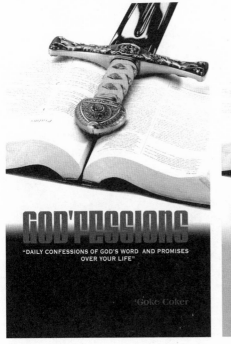